New Jersey's
Postsuburban Economy

PINPOINTS

Pinpoints is a series of concise books created to explore complex topics by explaining key theories, current scholarship, and important concepts in a brief, accessible style. Each Pinpoints book, in under 100 pages, enables readers to gain a working knowledge of essential topics quickly.

Written by leading Rutgers University faculty, the books showcase preeminent scholars from the humanities, social sciences, or sciences. Pinpoints books provide readers with access to world-class teaching and research faculty and offer a window to a broad range of subjects, for a wide circle of scholars, students, and nonspecialist general readers.

Rutgers University Press, through its groundbreaking Pinpoints series, brings affordable and quality educational opportunities to readers worldwide.

When complete, the series will comprise the following five volumes:

Deborah Carr, *Worried Sick: How Stress Hurts Us and How to Bounce Back*

Nicole Fleetwood, *On Racial Icons: Blackness and Public Imagination*

James W. Hughes and Joseph J. Seneca, *New Jersey's Postsuburban Economy*

Toby C. Jones, *Running Dry: Essays on Water and Environmental Crisis*

Charles Keeton, *A Ray of Light in a Sea of Dark Matter*

New Jersey's Postsuburban Economy

JAMES W. HUGHES
JOSEPH J. SENECA

RUTGERS UNIVERSITY PRESS

New Brunswick, New Jersey, and London

Library of Congress Control Number: 2014939602

ISBN: 978-0-8135-7000-6 (ePub)

Visit our website: http://rutgerspress.rutgers.edu

Manufactured in the United States of America

Contents

Figures

TABLES

Preface

THE ECONOMY OF NEW JERSEY, from its colonial origins to the present day, has continuously confronted the challenges and uncertainties of technological and demographic change. And it has always responded successfully, placing itself at the forefront of each national and global economic era.

In the seventeenth and eighteenth centuries, New Jersey's economy was largely rural agricultural and natural resources–based. By the late nineteenth and early twentieth centuries, the state had transformed itself into a leading-edge industrial behemoth, benefiting from its proximity to water and steam power, electricity, railroads, and urban manufacturing agglomeration. It adapted effectively to these new technology forces and successfully reinvented itself. As a result, New Jersey became a centerpiece of an urbanized, industrialized America.

By the late twentieth century, the state's economy had once again been completely transformed. Its older manufacturing base was obsolete in the new global environment. Responding to this challenge, New Jersey became a leading-edge postindustrial dynamo, building on its strengths: suburban highway office corridors, advanced information technology, the Internet, and knowledge-based services. Again, the state adapted to new technological and economic forces and successfully reinvented itself. New Jersey positioned itself at the forefront of America's suburbanized information-age, research-driven economy.

The emergence of the twentieth-century white-collar economy was underpinned by a key demographic that simultaneously transformed New Jersey from a predominantly urban state to a prominently suburban one: the huge postwar baby boom, the most suburban-centric generation in history. The locational preferences of this generation, along with key transportation investments, helped redefine the state's economic geography and its corporate landscape; the end result was one of America's strongest suburban economic agglomerations of automobile-dependent office employment, high-speed highways, and accompanying sprawling multidimensional residential suburbs.

But the baby boom will soon be yesterday's workforce. Tomorrow's workforce will be dominated by a new, expansive generation comprising echo boomers and millennials. Such young creatives—who came of age in the present-day, advanced digital-technology world—currently do not find the car-culture suburbs in which they grew up an attractive place to live, work, or play. Already, the locational preferences of corporate America are changing in parallel. Density, walkability, public transit, work-life balance, and urban amenities have grown significantly as quality-of-life locational attractions. Suddenly, New Jersey's greatest core advantage in the late twentieth century—a suburban-dominated, automobile-dependent economy and lifestyle—is regarded as a disadvantage.

The state once again faces the challenges and uncertainties of change. New Jersey will have to adapt and reinvent itself yet again—this time to a postsuburban digital economy that is being shaped by increasingly sophisticated mobile information technology and the workforce that employs it.

The purpose of this book is to describe the forces that are now propelling the state into yet another economic era. It does this in the context of historical economic transformations of New Jersey, setting out the technological, demographic, and transportation shifts that defined and drove them.

This work is heavily based on our nearly three-decade-long Rutgers Regional Report series that has analyzed multiple facets of New Jersey's economy, fiscal conditions, demography, business sectors, and housing markets vis-à-vis those of the nation and the broader region. That series is a microcosm of the transformation of New Jersey. It began in an era of writing manuscripts on typewriters and conducting ponderous data analysis on mainframe computers. It transitioned to exchanging floppy discs by getting in our cars and driving to meet colleagues midway between our homes so that we could continue to work on reports on the weekends. It moved to writing, researching, and exchanging draft reports by personal computer with high-powered Pentium chips, and has now evolved into producing an electronic book with intense but mostly virtual contact among writers, a research assistant, a senior production expert, and Rutgers University Press staff.

We are deeply grateful to Rutgers University for its support over the years of the Rutgers Regional Report series. We hope that the series has extended the recognition of the university throughout the policymaking community and to the larger, interested public.

We also thank the many individuals who have assisted us over this time in these reports and in the preparation of this book. Will Irving has provided careful and accurate research support for our work for nearly a decade. Arlene Pashman's impeccable work as production and senior editor has been invaluable. Thea Berkhout and Marcia Hannigan have assisted us in numerous ways to get this manuscript finished on time.

Finally, we gratefully acknowledge the encouragement of Marlie Wasserman, the director of Rutgers University Press, who persisted gently, but steadily, to convince us to integrate and extend the Rutgers Regional Reports into a coherent and new text. All errors and misinterpretations of the data and trends are solely those of the authors.

James W. Hughes
Joseph J. Seneca
March 2014

New Jersey's
Postsuburban Economy

CHAPTER 1

Introduction and Overview

IN AN ECONOMY AS dynamic and diverse as that of New Jersey, the only constant is change. In 1940, there were 1.3 million jobs in the state. By 2000, total employment had more than tripled to nearly four million jobs, but these were jobs of a much different nature.

An ever-expanding and evolving economy and sustained decade-by-decade job growth characterized the sixty-year period. But post-2000, a new dimension of change introduced itself. Unfortunately, it was negative change. By 2013, thirteen years later, total employment in the state had declined to 3.9 million jobs. The dynamics that had shaped the post–World War II twentieth-century economy of New Jersey underwent fundamental changes as the twenty-first century advanced.

COMPOSITIONAL SHIFTS

Change takes place not only in size but also in function and structure. A precolonial agrarian economy in New Jersey was ultimately supplanted by an urban-industrial goods-producing economy by the late nineteenth century, which, in turn, was replaced by a suburban postindustrial service economy by the late twentieth century. A goods-producing state was completely transformed to a service-providing state.

New Jersey was once primarily concerned with making things. Now it is primarily concerned with selling things and

I

servicing things and people. One metric of this transformation is the balance between goods producers and service providers:[1]

- In 1943, the state's economy had two goods producers for every single service provider.
- By 1962, there was one goods producer for every single service provider.
- By 1982, there was one goods producer for every two service providers.
- By 2013, there was one goods producer for nearly eight service providers.

This dramatic shift was due not only to the rapid growth of services but also to a virtual hemorrhage of manufacturing activity; almost three-quarters of the state's peak number of manufacturing jobs in 1969 had disappeared by 2013. A second set of metrics gauges the specific manufacturing–trade relationship:

- In 1943, the state's economy had 4.5 jobs in manufacturing compared with one job in trade (wholesale and retail).
- By 1963, there were two manufacturing jobs compared with one job in trade.
- By 1983, there was one manufacturing job compared with one job in trade.
- By 2013, there was one job in manufacturing compared with nearly three in trade.

Production had fully yielded to consumption—and to services, including advanced, highly sophisticated services. As a result of compositional changes during the last three decades, New Jersey now stands as a leading-edge exemplar of America's knowledge-dependent economy. Within the vast portfolio of services, the state currently has unique concentrations of employment in the following advanced sectors:

- Logistics and Distribution (technically wholesale trade, transportation, and warehousing)[2]
- Telecommunications (a subset of the broader information sector)
- Financial Activities
- Professional and Business Services (encompasses a diverse range of services)
- Corporate Headquarters (technically management of companies and enterprises)

These potent concentrations are the key locomotives of the state's twenty-first-century economy.

INCOME

The emergence of the new economy brought with it substantial income gains to New Jersey. In the 1980s, the state's per capita personal income was 16 percent higher than that of the nation (table 1.1). By 1990, it had surged to 26 percent higher; it increased further to 28 percent higher by 2000. But it then slipped to 26 percent higher by 2012. Nonetheless, this income advantage is indicative of the high productivity and quality of the state's employment base.

However, lack of employment growth in New Jersey post-2000 has resulted in an erosion in the state's strong share of the total personal income of the United States. New Jersey accounts for 2.8 percent of the nation's population. Other things being equal, that should be the guide as to the state's expected share of the nation's personal income. But in 2000, the state accounted for 3.8 percent, indicating a strong income concentration tied to New Jersey's much higher per capita income (see table 1.1). Between 2000 and 2012, the state's income share slipped to 3.6 percent. Despite declining in relative income advantage and in share, New Jersey is still well positioned on these key economic metrics.

TABLE 1.1

Total Personal Income, New Jersey and the United States 1980–2012

Year	New Jersey Share of Total National Personal Income	Ratio: NJ Per Capita Income to Nation
1980	3.8	1.16
1990	3.9	1.26
2000	3.8	1.28
2012	3.6	1.26

SOURCE: U.S. Bureau of Economic Analysis.

DEMOGRAPHICS

From the end of World War II and into the second decade of the current century, two other sustained and fundamental changes took place—in demography—that also helped to continually reshape the New Jersey economy. The postwar youth society ultimately became the middle-aged society and then the mature society—all defined by the life-cycle stages of the fabled baby boom generation. Now it is being challenged by a second youth society defined by the echo boom generation, newly ascendant in the labor force.[3] Baby boomers represent the workforce of the past, echo boomers the workforce of the future.

Similarly, at the end of World War II, New Jersey was dominated by a white population, with a small cadre of minority groups; today, New Jersey is one of the most diverse states in the country, with more than one of five citizens foreign born.[4] This is a second dimension of the workforce of the future.

SPATIAL TRANSFORMATION

The reinvention of the New Jersey economy proceeded in lockstep with an unprecedented tidal wave of decentralization and suburbanization during the second half of the twentieth century—an initial decentralization of population and housing, followed by retailing, and then by all sectors of a once highly centralized urban-based economy. The state's manufacturing-centric central cities suffered enormously in potency and scale. The vast new knowledge-based postindustrial activities were largely housed in office buildings, the factory floors of the new economy. By 2000, New Jersey had one of the greatest agglomerations of suburban office space in the United States, filled with legions of baby boom workers, who lived a totally suburban-centric life.

Much of the vast office inventory was located in suburban highway-oriented growth corridors. New Jersey was a nation-leading example for this automobile-dependent development format. It was the nation's cutting-edge growth model—it was the state's core economic competency and specialization. The nets of suburban growth corridors reached their greatest concentration in the narrow six-county midsection of the state known as the New Jersey Wealth Belt. It was assumed that they represented the skeletal framework of the state's twentieth-first-century economy. However, that assumption was soon proved wrong.

Changing Dynamics

A number of forces emerged post-2000 to force another change on the New Jersey economy. The new demographics—ascendant echo boomers/millennials—exhibit a much greater preference for high-density, transit-centric environments in which to live, work, and play; isolated, one dimensional suburban office campuses have minimal allure. What may be emerging is a new demographic–economic synergy. What millennials want—sense of place, walkability, urban amenities, and public transit—are the same qualities that corporate America now seeks. A new era of corporate urbanism appears to be under way.

Concurrently, increasingly sophisticated information technology redefined the very nature of knowledge-based work, redefined the very function of office buildings, redefined productivity and the shape of the economy. Corporate cultures and business models have been radically transformed. Innovation, creativity, interaction, and collaboration are now the key white-collar functions. Formerly standardized work protocols have been made obsolete by advanced information technologies. The sheer severity of the Great 2007–09 Recession and its aftermath has accelerated a transformation that had been well under way. Information technology and globalization have also slowed the growth of knowledge-based jobs, both nationwide and in New Jersey, changing the very foundation of office-space demand. Corporate America is engaged in space deleveraging, shrinking its vast office inventory.

Moreover, increasingly sophisticated mobile information technology is unshackling/untethering workers from fixed-in-place systems and their umbilical cords. This has resulted in threshold increases in worker mobility, redefining and extending the spatial boundaries of the traditional workplace. New Jersey's once world-famous suburban office corridors started to represent the geography of the past. There is a fundamental spatial reorganization of the New Jersey economy taking place, with the outer suburban office footprint contracting. The suburbanization forces that shaped New Jersey for a half century have been disrupted by this confluence of events.

This does not mean that the economy of suburban New Jersey is destined to stagnate in this new environment. Nor does it mean that we will have echo boomer–free office corridors. But it does strongly suggest that business as usual is not an option. Offices will still be central to the knowledge-based economy of the future. There remains a vast inventory of past physical office investment in New Jersey. A major imperative is to reimagine such existing assets, adapting them to the new economic normal. Significant strides have been made already, but there is a long road to completion of the successfully retooled economic infrastructure that a twenty-first-century economy requires.

ORGANIZATION

Chapter 2 examines New Jersey in the context of the broader national business cycle that caused sharp changes in the state's economic trajectory twenty-two times between World War II and 2014. Each cyclical period is briefly analyzed in terms of its impact on employment expansion and contraction in the state. The chapter then presents the current structure and composition of the New Jersey economy, with particular attention to the state's unique employment concentrations by business sector compared with the nation. Chapter 3 reviews the broad historical origins of the state's economy and the major transformations and periods of development that have evolved from its original agrarian base. It details fundamental historical pivot points and then examines the postwar periods of economic–geographic change. To illustrate the dramatic regional transformation of New Jersey since World War II, direct decade-by-decade periods of comparison to New York City are detailed.

Much of the change in the state's economy over time has been tied to transportation. Chapter 4 examines the strong linkages between transportation systems and the patterns of economic growth and presents a detailed look at New Jersey's successive nation-leading transportation eras. The final geographic expression of the state's suburban office-based knowledge economy when the twentieth century came to a close was the Wealth Belt, comprising six counties of North Central New Jersey. Its development, and the changes in other regions within the state to the present, is the subject of chapter 5.

Chapter 6 explores two additional key forces that have continuously shaped and reshaped the New Jersey economy over time: demographics and housing. Demographically driven periods or eras of housing development are defined, and the key demographic sectors that will further reshape the economy in the future are examined. Finally, chapter 7 presents the dynamics that are currently redefining yet again New Jersey's economy and geography. The future of the state's knowledge-based economy will be linked to the future of its massive suburban office inventory.

All data are current as of March 2014. Data revisions are continually taking place, so the reader is cautioned. However, the broad trends derived from the data should not be affected significantly.

CHAPTER 2

The Structure of the New Jersey Economy and the Business Cycle

OVER THE PAST 150 YEARS, New Jersey has experienced two major economic transformations, each time successfully reinventing itself. At the end of the nineteenth century, the state's once dominant agricultural economy had been supplanted by a powerful technology-driven urban manufacturing economy. At the end of the twentieth century, the state's manufacturing economy had been supplanted by a powerful technology-driven, knowledge-based, suburban service economy. Now, in a vast temporal telescoping, in the second decade of the twenty-first century the state faces a third economic transformation involving its demography, its competitive core advantages, and its residential choices. That transformation will be examined more fully in subsequent chapters of this book. This chapter focuses on what has transpired in the state during the business cycles of the second half of the twentieth century and then presents the current structure and composition of the New Jersey economy.

STRUCTURAL VERSUS CYCLICAL ECONOMIC SHIFTS

The cusp of the twenty-first-century New Jersey economy was the end result of two broad, large-scale structural shifts that took place during the nineteenth and twentieth centuries, each of which placed the state in nation-leading positions. First was the shift from a preindustrial-, agricultural-, and natural resources–based economic foundation to an urban industrial manufacturing one. This was followed by an equally profound shift to a postindustrial information-age service economy. These major transformations and their impact on the state were further shaped by secondary structural shifts as well as the expansionary and contractionary (recessionary) stages of the business cycle.

A number of secondary structural shifts have taken place since the end of World War II. These are examined in later chapters, but it is useful to itemize them briefly in terms of their underlying forces and dynamics.

- The housing needs of returning World War II veterans unleashed an unprecedented tidal wave of residential suburbanization across America. Being the suburban catchment area for both New York City and Philadelphia, New Jersey was the destination of vast urban middle-class migrations. The state was one of the epicenters of the emergence of automobile-dependent suburban America.

- Within newly built tract-house suburbia, a great baby boom erupted. The now fabled baby boom was that huge generation born between 1946 and 1964. Given the monumental scale of its suburbs, New Jersey became Baby Boom Central. Catering to the baby boom's needs at each of its life-cycle stages became a powerful, sustained economic force for the state for the remainder of the century.

- Housing construction, baby boom–inspired school construction, retail construction, and the production of all of the consumer goods that suburbia craved dominated New Jersey through 1970. Following the Great

Depression and World War II, the enormous pent-up demand for consumption and spending helped the economy soar.

- However, during the 1970s, domestic and international competition started to weaken the state's manufacturing base as new patterns of regional growth emerged. The rise of America's Sunbelt quickly became a media catchphrase, and the entire Northeast region began to lag. Two unprecedented oil crises were economic game changers.

- While suburban growth slowed, urban decline intensified. New Jersey's aging cities, beset by blight, saw their population losses accelerate. Demographic boom was supplanted by demographic bust. Following the baby boom was the baby-bust generation, an undersized population cohort born between 1965 and 1976. Demographic expansion had significant positive economic effects; demographic contraction had significant negative economic effects.

- Following the earlier established residential model, the suburbanization of the emergent knowledge-based economy swept through New Jersey during the 1980s and 1990s. Suburban office corridors became America's new growth model. The state was again at the national forefront; one of the greatest suburban office agglomerations in America emerged in New Jersey at this time.

- However, a housing-price bubble amid a widespread real estate frenzy engulfed the state in the 1980s, and the telecommunications/Internet bubble helped shape the 1990s. The initial positive economic effects of these two bubbles ultimately succumbed to the painful contractions that ensued.

- New Jersey was also a prime immigration destination during this period as the foreign-born population surged. At the same time, the second great population bulge of the postwar period emerged: the baby boom echo, those born between 1977 and 1995.

As these broad dynamics and shifts helped shape the great postindustrial transformation, the business cycle remained in full force, causing sharp changes in the state's economic trajectory twenty-two times between World War II and 2014.

CYCLICAL ECONOMIC CHANGES

Starting with the 1948–49 slump (the first postwar recession), there have been eleven recessions and eleven expansions in the post–World War II era, with the eleventh expansion currently in progress. Table 2.1 defines the month-to-month boundaries for these cycles, along with the total employment change for each. The lengths of the recession and expansion periods for the United States are defined by the National Bureau of Economic Research and are determined by a number of comprehensive economic measures.[1] Because there is less comprehensive data available at the state level, the phases of the business cycle for New Jersey can generally be defined by employment peaks and troughs.[2] Generally there has been close correspondence between the two, but recently there have been significant divergences.

RECESSION LENGTH

The average length of America's postwar recessions has been 11.1 months (table 2.1). The shortest was only six months (1980). The longest was eighteen months (2007–09); the second longest was sixteen months, the length of both the 1973–75 and 1981–82 downturns. The last national recession—the Great Recession (December 2007 to June 2009)—was not only the longest, but also by far the deepest in terms of absolute job loss (7,406,000 jobs).[3]

TABLE 2.1

Length of New Jersey Employment Downturns vs. National Recessions since World War II
(Total nonfarm employment, seasonally adjusted, in thousands)

NEW JERSEY DOWNTURN			NATIONAL RECESSION		
Month-to-Month Period[a,d]	Duration	Employment Change	Month-to-Month Period[c]	Duration	Employment Change
July 1948–July 1949	12 months	-91	November 1948–October 1949	11 months	-2,244
August 1953–August 1954	12 months	-49	July 1953–May 1954	10 months	-1,571
March 1957–May 1958	14 months	-88	August 1957–April 1958	8 months	-2,099
May 1960–February 1961	9 months	-25	April 1960–February 1961	10 months	-1,256
April 1970–April 1971	12 months	-26	December 1969–November 1970	11 months	-831
May 1974–May 1975	12 months	-134	November 1973–March 1975	16 months	-1,263
March 1980–July 1980	4 months	-22	January 1980–July 1980	6 months	-965
September 1981–April 1982	7 months	-25	July 1981–November 1982	16 months	-2,819
March 1989–April 1992	37 months	-260	July 1990–March 1991	8 months	-1,256
December 2000–July 2002	19 months	-61	March 2001–November 2001	8 months	-1,581
January 2008–September 2010[b]	32 months	-257	December 2007–June 2009	18 months	-7,406
Average:	15.5 months	-94	Average:	11.1 months	-2,117

(continued)

TABLE 2.1

Length of New Jersey Employment Upturns vs. National Expansions since World War II
(Total nonfarm employment, seasonally adjusted, in thousands) (continued)

NEW JERSEY UPTURN[c]			NATIONAL EXPANSION[c]		
Month-to-Month Period[d]	Duration	Employment Change	Month-to-Month Period[e]	Duration	Employment Change
July 1949–August 1953	49 months	285	October 1949–July 1953	45 months	7,586
August 1954–March 1957	31 months	173	May 1954–August 1957	39 months	4,161
May 1958–May 1960	24 months	129	April 1958–April 1960	24 months	3,785
February 1961–April 1970	110 months	615	February 1961–December 1969	106 months	17,684
April 1971–May 1974	37 months	217	November 1970–November 1973	36 months	7,503
May 1975–March 1980	58 months	398	March 1975–January 1980	58 months	14,153
July 1980–September 1981	14 months	61	July 1980–July 1981	12 months	1,765
April 1982–March 1989	83 months	622	November 1982–July 1990	92 months	21,050
April 1992–December 2000	104 months	579	March 1991–March 2001	120 months	24,164
July 2002–January 2008	66 months	129	November 2001–December 2007	73 months	7,190
September 2010– Dec. 2013	39 months	93	June 2009–Current (Dec. 2013)	54 months	6,451
Average:	57.6 months	321	Average:	60.5 months	10,904

(continued)

TABLE 2.1 *(continued)*

NOTES:

a. Periods are from end of month to end of month.

b. New Jersey's private-sector employment reached its cyclical trough in February 2010. However, public-sector employment continued to decline sporadically, resulting in multiple short-term troughs for total employment. Accordingly, September 2010 was used as the cyclical trough for total nonfarm employment.

c. New Jersey Upturn and National Expansion averages for Duration and Employment Change exclude the most recent, ongoing periods.

d. New Jersey periods are determined from seasonally adjusted employment data.

e. National periods based on economic output data.

SOURCES:
New Jersey: New Jersey Department of Labor; U.S. Bureau of Labor Statistics, New York Office.
United States: National Bureau of Economic Research; U.S. Bureau of Labor Statistics.

In contrast, New Jersey's average downturn in its eleven recessions (15.5 months) was longer than that of the nation. There was little variation between New Jersey and the United States during the first seven postwar recessions; their corresponding lengths were reasonably consistent. However, the next two recessions showed substantial divergence. The length (seven months) of the state's eighth downturn (1981–82) was less than half that (sixteen months) of the nation. New Jersey's mild setback contrasted sharply with a nation experiencing, at the time, its worst recession since the Great Depression. The reverse happened during the next (ninth) cyclical downturn. The state's thirty-seven-month-long 1989–92 decline was its worst since the Great Depression, while the eight-month duration of the national recession was well below average. It was the sheer length of this New Jersey downturn that led to a much higher overall average length of recessions in the state.

The next two downturns introduced a new variation. Until this point, the official national recession dates generally corresponded to the dates of national employment peaks and troughs. However, this close relationship has disappeared. During the last two contractions, employment continued to decline following the end of the recession. This led to the phrase "jobless economic growth." For example, the tenth recession (2001) was technically shorter (eight months) nationally than in New Jersey (nineteen months). However, employment losses in the nation continued for another twenty-one months (to August 2003) after the recession technically ended in November 2001.

EXPANSION LENGTH

The average length (60.5 months) of the eleven economic expansions in the United States was slightly more than five years (table 2.1). New Jersey's average length (57.6 months) was slightly shorter. In all of the expansions, the national–state differential was minor, with the 1991–2001 expansion representing the largest variation. This was due to the extraordinary length of New Jersey's 1989–92 recession, which delayed the start of the state's economic recovery until 1992. The differential was almost as large during the current expansion; part of this was due to the nation's extended period of job-loss economic growth following the technical end of the downturn.

THE GREAT UPS AND DOWNS

Three great growth cycles dominated the past sixty years: 1961–69/(1970); 1982–90/(1989); and 1991(1992)–2001(2000).[4] In each, the employment gains were nearly double those of the "average" expansion (see table 2.1). The worst of all of the postwar recessions in New Jersey was the 1989–92 downturn. The Great 2007–09 Recession was by far the worst national contraction.

A DETAILED LOOK AT
RECENT PATTERNS

Moving through the boom-bust phases of the business cycle during the past three decades is analogous to a wild ride on an economic roller coaster. Since 1980, New Jersey and the United States have experienced dizzying ascents and dramatic falls. Technically, there have been five business-cycle expansions and four business-cycle contractions (or recessions.) Two of the expansions were of record magnitude and length, but two of the contractions were the worst downturns since the Great Depression. Thus, New Jersey has passed through two great economic booms and two great economic busts since 1980, each of which was a transformative event.

Annual change in private-sector payroll employment is an effective metric for viewing the pattern of the recent business cycle over time (1980–2013). The United States cycle is examined first to provide context, followed by that of New Jersey. The state certainly reflects all stages of the national economic cycle—recessions (contractions) and expansions—although there are differences in relative order of magnitude.

THE UNITED STATES

Annual growth or decline in private-sector employment for the United States is presented in figure 2.1.[5] As a point of reference for evaluating the initial base years (1980–82) of the chart, it should be pointed out that both of the global energy crises that took place in the 1970s precipitated subsequent economic slowdowns and severe recessions. The 1973 oil shock produced the 1973–75 recession, at that time the worst economic downturn since the Great Depression.[6] Then the 1979 oil crisis ultimately led to the more severe 1981–82 recession, which became the *new* worst economic downturn since the Great Depression.[7]

As shown in figure 2.1, there were two years of tepid employment growth—1980 (+77,000 jobs) and 1981 (+250,000 jobs)—resulting from the 1979 oil shock. Then, the nation lost just over two million jobs in 1982, a painful loss reflecting the severity of the 1981–82 recession. This was a manufacturing-centric contraction, as the economy's industrial sector adjusted to a new era of high energy costs and growing international competition.

Recovery then ensued, with the economy shifting into postindustrial, office-based service activities on a broad scale.[8] The expansion started with extraordinarily high employment growth in 1983 (+3.4 million jobs) and 1984 (+3.6 million jobs), a rapid start followed by positive employment gains through 1989. This expansion turned out to be the longest peacetime expansion in the nation's history.[9] A mild recession then followed, with employment losses experienced in 1990 (-82,000 jobs) and 1991 (-1.0 million jobs).[10]

What emerged from this shallow downturn was the longest economic expansion in history: 120 months, or a full ten years.[11] Although it technically started in 1991, the first year of employment growth was 1992 (+933,000 jobs). From this

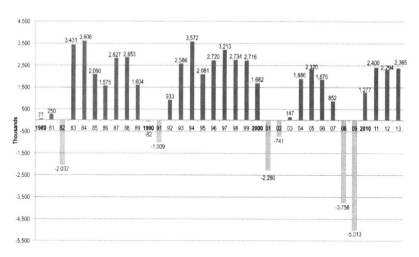

2.1. U.S. Private-Sector Employment Change,
Annual Change (December to December), 1980–2013
Source: U.S. Bureau of Labor Statistics.

slow start, the economy then gathered substantial momentum as knowledge-based, information-age activities soared. For seven straight years (1993–99), the economy had an average annual employment gain of approximately 2.8 million jobs, and in two of those years job gains exceeded three million (1994 and 1997). It was the greatest employment-growth period in the nation's history.

In the latter 1990s, advancing information technologies—particularly the Internet, high-powered desktop computers, and fiber-optic connectivity—spurred robust capital investment, a surging stock market, and new business models, giving added longevity to the expansion. This marked the final stages of an extraordinary job-growth period at the end of the twentieth century. Between November 1982 and March 2001, the nation had experienced two great expansions: 1982–90, the longest peacetime expansion in the nation's history, and 1991–2001, the longest expansion ever. The two were interrupted only by the mild 1990–91 recession. Approximately thirty-nine million private-sector

jobs were added during the 1982–2001 era—a record period of
sustained employment expansion—lending a high degree of optimism about the new millennium economy to come.[12]

Unfortunately, what actually transpired proved to be quite different. The information-technology boom ultimately succumbed
to excess and was supplanted by an information-technology
bust. The "go-go" years of the 1990s transitioned to the "no-go"
years of the 2000s. In 2001, the nation shed nearly 2.3 million
jobs, and in 2002 another 741,000 jobs were lost.[13] While an
employment turnaround finally took place in 2003 (+147,000
jobs), the expansion never really gained full traction, despite the
housing and credit bubbles that dominated the post-9/11 years.
As is evident from the small scale of the employment gains of the
2003–07 period in figure 2.1, only in 2005 did job growth sur-
pass the two million level. It did so seven times in the expansion
of the 1990s, and five times during the expansions of the 1980s.
Thus, the 2003–07 employment gains were extraordinarily weak
compared with those of its two immediate predecessors.

The bursting of the housing and credit bubbles led to the
Great 2007–09 Recession, yet again a new worst downturn since
the Great Depression.[14] At eighteen months in length, it was
the longest downturn since the Great Depression. The previous
post-Depression record recession duration was sixteen months,
the length of the 1981–82 recession.[15] The annual employment
losses of the Great Recession were nothing less than staggering.
In 2008, the nation lost 3.8 million jobs; this was surpassed by a
wide margin in 2009, when five million jobs were lost. Payroll
employment statistics were first compiled in 1939. In the full
history of the data series to date, the losses experienced in 2009
were greater than those of any other year.

Employment finally started to recover modestly in 2010 (+1.3
million jobs) and then averaged over 2.3 million new jobs annually
for the next three years. While somewhat stronger to date than the
2003–07 expansion, the starting point of the current economic

recovery was from an employment deficit of record depth stemming from the severity of the Great Recession and its aftermath.

NEW JERSEY

In the first seven business-cycle contractions following World War II, New Jersey's employment declines aligned quite closely with the nation in both relative scale and duration. However, the state's 1981–82 recession turned out to be quite different. While the nation experienced its worst recession since the Great Depression (lasting a far-above-average sixteen months), New Jersey's recession was barely visible. It lasted just seven months, and the state lost only a minuscule 4,900 jobs in 1982 (figure 2.2).[16] New Jersey had already suffered significant manufacturing employment losses during the decade of the 1970s, so it was not affected as much by the recession's sharp national manufacturing contraction.

New Jersey also got an earlier start in the transformation to a postindustrial knowledge-based, information-age economy due to its highly educated workforce and the suburbanization of economic activity from New York City. At the same time, the state was a leading-edge participant in the real estate boom in the 1980s.[17] As a result, the expansion started in 1983 with the greatest employment-growth year in New Jersey's history (+148,300 jobs), followed by the second largest in 1984 (+132,300 jobs). The growth of knowledge-based office jobs and their physical shelter in office buildings were the forces that drove the entire expansion. However, severe office overbuilding, a home-price bubble, and other excesses ultimately led to the 1989–92 recession in the state—what became and remains New Jersey's worst downturn since the Great Depression. This represented a second diversion from the national pattern, since the United States experienced only a relatively minor recession in 1990–91. While the nation's downturn was only eight months long, New Jersey's downturn lasted fully thirty-seven months.

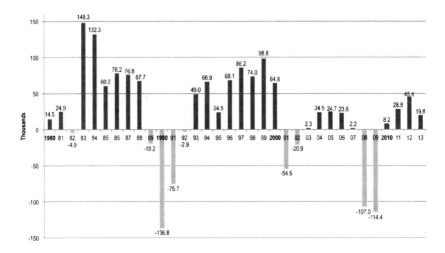

2.2 New Jersey Private-Sector Employment Change,
Annual Change (December to December), 1980–2013
SOURCE: U.S. Bureau of Labor Statistics.

The subsequent expansion's first full growth year was 1993 (+49,000 jobs), and the state lagged significantly behind the nation. But the second half of the decade (1996–2000) was characterized by strong employment growth. New Jersey was one of the epicenters of the information technology boom, led by the state's telecommunications industry. It reached its pinnacle with the massive investment related to the anticipated Y2K problem.[18] However, the technological boom turned to technological bust in 2001.

New Jersey's employment downturn in 2001–02 matched that of the nation, extending far beyond the technical end of the recession in November 2001. However, the state's subsequent 2003–07 expansion proved far weaker than the weak national expansion. The strongest employment growth year was 2004 (+24,500 jobs). To put this in context, the high-growth year of the 1990s expansion was 1999. Its 98,800 job gain was four

times as great as that of 2004. The high-growth year (1983) of the
1980s expansion had a job gain (+148,300) six times greater. So
the 2003–07 period could be interpreted as the expansion that
almost never was.

The Great 2007–09 Recession in New Jersey paralleled that
of the nation. The employment losses of 2009 (-114,400 jobs)
and 2008 (-107,000 jobs) were, respectively, the second and third
worst on record in the state. Only the 1990 loss (-136,800 jobs)
was greater.[19] The subsequent expansion started slowly in 2010
(+8,200 jobs). The employment gain of 2011 (+28,800 jobs) was
three and a half times as great as that of 2010, and the 2012
increase (+45,400 jobs) was one and a half times as large as that
of 2011. Thus, a strong trend appeared to be in effect, but in 2013
employment growth faltered.

Another perspective of New Jersey's economic roller
coaster ride is detailed in figure 2.3, which presents the expansions and contractions precisely dated to the monthly starting
and end points as defined by the National Bureau of Economic
Research. The two great expansions—April 1982 to March 1989
(+622,400 jobs) and April 1992 to December 2000 (+578,500
jobs)—stand in sharp contrast to the new millennium expansions—July 2002 to January 2008 (+128,700 jobs) and September 2010 to December 2013 (+93,200). It is also evident that
the employment losses (-256,600) of the Great Recession in
the state (January 2008 to September 2010) completely erased
the gains (+128,700 jobs) of the preceding 2002–08 expansion. The three earlier recessions—including the record March
1989 to April 1992 downturn—erased only a portion of the job
gains of the preceding expansions. New Jersey has just passed
through the most difficult business cycle stage that it has ever
experienced.

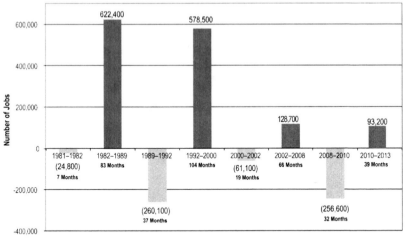

2.3 New Jersey's Economic Roller Coaster. (Employment Change for Periods Indicated)
Source: New Jersey Department of Labor.

The Structure and Composition of the New Jersey Economy

The business cycle and structural shifts have culminated in the state's current economy. Its basic structure, as well as a New Jersey–U.S. comparison, is detailed in tables 2.2 and 2.3. The industries that make up the economy are defined by the North American Industry Classification System (NAICS). The broad classifications take the following form:

Total Employment

    Total Private Sector

        Goods Producing

            Mining and Logging

            Construction

            Manufacturing

Private Service Providing

    Trade, Transportation, and Utilities

    Information

    Financial Activities

    Professional and Business Services

    Education and Health Services

    Leisure and Hospitality

    Other Services

GOVERNMENT

    Federal Government

    State Government

    Local Government

Total employment is partitioned into two major groups—total private sector and government. The private sector has two large components—goods producing and private service providing. Goods-producing activities comprise three major subcategories that are technically known as supersectors: mining and logging, construction, and manufacturing. Private service-providing activities have seven supersectors: trade, transportation, and utilities; information; financial activities; professional and business services; education and health services; leisure and hospitality; and other services. Government has three supersectors: federal, state, and local. All of the supersectors have multiple subsectors and further detailed subcategories.

New Jersey's basic employment structure in 2013 using these industrial classifications is presented in table 2.2. Several additional subsectors that are particularly important in defining the state's knowledge-based economy are also detailed. The table includes both absolute numbers of jobs in each sector and their share of total. New Jersey's total employment in 2013 was just under four million jobs; 3.3 million (84.1 percent) were in the

TABLE 2.2

New Jersey Employment Shares by Sector, 2013

(Annual averages in thousands, nonseasonally adjusted)

	Total	Share(%)
TOTAL NONFARM	3,955.4	100.0
TOTAL PRIVATE SECTOR	3,327.7	84.1
GOODS PRODUCING	382.6	9.7
Mining and Logging	1.2	0.0
Construction	133.3	3.4
Manufacturing	248.1	6.3
Durable Goods	113.6	2.9
Non-Durable Goods	134.5	3.4
PRIVATE SERVICE PROVIDING	2,945.1	74.5
Trade, Transportation & Utilities	835.1	21.1
Wholesale Trade	213.2	5.4
Retail Trade	455.5	11.5
Transportation, Warehousing, and Utilities	166.4	4.2
Information	75.1	1.9
Financial Activities	250.5	6.3
Finance and Insurance	194.7	4.9
Real Estate and Rental and Leasing	55.8	1.4
Professional and Business Services	624.3	15.8
Professional, Scientific & Technical Services	281.2	7.1
Management of Companies and Enterprises	81.6	2.1
Adm./Support, Waste Mgt./Re-mediation Services	261.5	6.6

(continued)

TABLE 2.2

New Jersey Employment Shares by Sector, 2013 (continued)

	Total	Share (%)
Educational and Health Services	640.5	16.2
Educational Services	100.3	2.5
Health Care and Social Assistance	540.2	13.7
Leisure and Hospitality	353.9	8.9
Arts, Entertainment, and Recreation	57.7	1.5
Accommodation and Food Services	296.2	7.5
Other Services	165.9	4.2
GOVERNMENT	627.6	15.9
Federal Government	48.3	1.2
State Government	145.6	3.7
Local Government	433.7	11.0

NOTE: North American Industry Classification (NAICS) employment sectors.
SOURCE: New Jersey Department of Labor.

private sector, and 627,600 (15.9 percent) were in the public sector. The largest private supersectors were trade, transportation, and utilities (835,100 jobs); education and health services (640,500 jobs); and professional and business services (624,300 jobs). More than one-half (53.1 percent) of all jobs in New Jersey are in these three supersectors. In the government sector (627,600 jobs), local government (433,700 jobs) predominates. How does this basic composition compare with that of the nation?

Table 2.3 provides the employment profile (percentage shares) in 2013 for New Jersey and the United States. For each sector, New Jersey's share of the nation's employment in that sector is also presented. As a point of reference, in 2013 New Jersey accounted for 2.9 percent of the total job base of the United States. If the state has a higher share in any industrial category, that would indicate an representation or a

TABLE 2.3

Sector Employment, 2013

Percentage Distribution and New Jersey Share of United States

Sector	Employment Distribution		NJ Share of U.S. (%)
	NJ (%)	U.S. (%)	
TOTAL NONFARM	100.0	100.0	2.9
TOTAL PRIVATE SECTOR	84.1	84.0	2.9
GOODS PRODUCING	9.7	13.7	2.0
Mining and Logging	0.0	0.6	0.1
Construction	3.4	4.3	2.3
Manufacturing	6.3	8.8	2.1
PRIVATE SERVICE PROVIDING	74.5	70.3	3.1
Trade, Transportation, & Utilities	21.1	19.0	3.2
Wholesale Trade	5.4	4.2	3.7
Retail Trade	11.5	11.1	3.0
Transportation, Warehousing, and Utilities	4.2	3.7	3.3
Information	1.9	2.0	2.8
Publishing Industries (except Internet)	0.5	0.5	2.8
Telecommunications	0.8	0.6	3.7
Internet Service Providers, Web Portals, Data Processing Services	0.2	0.2	2.8
Financial Activities	6.3	5.8	3.2
Professional and Business Services	15.8	13.6	3.4
Professional, Scientific, and Technical Services	7.1	6.0	3.5
Management of Companies and Enterprises	2.1	1.5	3.9
Educational and Health Services	16.2	15.5	3.0

(continued)

TABLE 2.3

Sector Employment, 2013
Percentage Distribution and New Jersey Share of United States
(continued)

Sector	Employment Distribution		NJ Share of U.S. (%)
	NJ (%)	U.S. (%)	
Leisure and Hospitality	8.9	10.4	2.5
Other Services	4.2	4.0	3.0
GOVERNMENT	15.9	16.0	2.9
Federal Government	1.2	2.0	1.7
State Government	3.7	3.7	2.9
Local Government	11.0	10.3	3.1

SOURCE: U.S. Bureau of Labor Statistics.

concentration/specialization. A lower share would indicate an underrepresentation.

New Jersey's goods-producing activities account for just 2.0 percent of those of the nation, indicating a significant under-representation. They account for just 9.7 percent of the state's total employment, compared with a 13.7 percent share in the nation. Thus, New Jersey can no longer be classified as a major goods producing state. It has very little mining activity, accounting for only 0.1 percent of the nation's mining employment, and is significantly underrepresented in both construction (a 2.3 percent share) and manufacturing (a 2.1 percent share).

This pattern across the three goods-producing supersectors is not surprising. The state has few natural resources industries; its population is growing far slower than that of the nation, so its population-dependent construction activities, such as housing and local retail, are also below the national average in size; and its economic

transformation has left it with a relatively small manufacturing base.
Once the state's major economic activity, manufacturing accounted
for only 6.3 percent of the state's total employment in 2013. This
compares with 8.8 percent in the nation. Thus, the state's historic
blue-collar image is a relic of the distant past.

New Jersey has become a major private service-providing
state, accounting for 3.1 percent of the nation's total service-
providing employment. The state's economy is overrepresented
in trade, transportation, and utilities (a 3.2 percent share of the
nation), reflecting its outsized role in logistics and warehousing
and its high-income consumer household base. New Jersey is
the third-largest warehouse distribution market in the country. It
accounts for 3.7 percent of the nation's wholesale trade employment and 3.3 percent of the nation's transportation, warehousing,
and utilities employment. The information supersector in New
Jersey—which has a 2.8 percent share—is almost in line with the
nation, but the state has a major concentration in its telecommunications subsector, which has a 3.7 percent share. This reflects the
state's long-standing position in this industry, which started with
AT&T's historically strong presence in New Jersey. Major shifts
and changes in that industry and the decline of landline communications have eroded New Jersey's former dominance. New
opportunities in the industry have been created, and significant
changes within the structure of the industry are under way.

The state also has a major concentration in two supersectors
that serve as primary tenants for the state's vast office inventory:
financial activities, and professional and business services. Financial activities account for 3.2 percent of the nation's employment
in this sector, making the state a major financial center. The
same is true of the large and diverse professional and business
services sector (3.4 percent). It has particularly strong concentrations in two of its subsectors: professional, scientific, and technical services; and management of companies and enterprises.
Management of companies and enterprises comprises mainly

corporate headquarters activities. New Jersey has 3.9 percent of the nation's employment in this subsector, more than one-third greater than its share of total national employment (2.9 percent). "Professional, scientific, and technical services" consists of such activities as legal, accounting, engineering, management, advertising, and research and development services. The state has 3.5 percent of the nation's jobs in this subsector.

New Jersey also has a major presence in educational and health services, and "other" services, both of which have 3.0 percent national shares, but is significantly underrepresented in the leisure and hospitality supersector (a 2.5 percent share).

New Jersey's total government employment accounts for 2.9 percent of that of the nation, suggesting that the state matches the nation exactly. However, that is not actually the case. The state has a greater than expected share (3.1 percent) of the nation's total local government employment.[20] Thus, New Jersey has more local government compared with the rest of the nation. New Jersey's state government employment has a 2.9 percent share, perfectly in line with its share of total U.S. employment, but is significantly underrepresented in the nation's civilian federal employment. New Jersey accounts for only 1.7 percent of federal government employment, which over time has had a diminishing presence and economic impact in the state.

New Jersey's strong employment profile is evident when each sector's share of the state's economy is compared with each sector's share of the national economy. Compared with the United States, New Jersey has greater shares of its economy in trade, transportation, and utilities (21.1 percent versus 19.0 percent), in educational and health services (16.2 percent versus 15.5 percent), professional and business services (15.8 percent versus 13.6 percent), and in financial activities (6.3 percent versus 5.8 percent). These are the key specialized sectors of the state's postindustrial economy, the evolution of which is narrated in the next chapter.

CHAPTER 3

_____

The Broad Historical
Evolution

_____

ECONOMIC ERAS

The demographic–economic geography of New Jersey as the twenty-first century commenced was the product of five decades of large-scale residential suburbanization, four decades of large-scale retail decentralization, and two decades of large-scale office and service industry deconcentration.[1] The dominant feature that emerged on the economic landscape was the suburban Wealth Belt—fully analyzed in chapter 5—the end result of this long trajectory of post–World War II geographic spread. Moreover, it is also the latest phase of an even longer historical record of spatial reorganization.

The New Jersey economy has continuously reinvented itself during the past two centuries, both structurally and spatially. Early settlements based on water-powered manufacturing and milling facilities scattered sparsely throughout a rural agricultural-based geography yielded to densely concentrated railroad- and steam-based urban production complexes that, in turn, succumbed to freeway-based "edge cities" sheltering the new information-age economy. Thus, there have been spatial advances and spatial withdrawals as cycles of technological innovation and industrial revolution have continuously renewed the New Jersey economy. The late twentieth century experienced a vast reshaping as dramatic as that of the late nineteenth century, when urbanization and city building reigned. Yet again, another profound transformation was in process as the second decade of the twenty-first century unfolded.

THE BROAD HISTORICAL RECORD

The history of New Jersey during the past two centuries has been characterized by continuous geographic movements and the emergence of new spatial concentrations and deconcentrations of people and economic activity. This evolution has been spurred by technological and economic change, along with demographic and social shifts. The state has moved from dispersed small settlements (early nineteenth century) based on water power and agriculture, to highly concentrated urban-industrial nodes (early twentieth century) predicated on steam power and railroads, to a vast Wealth Belt (late twentieth century) tied to an information-age economy. Then, unbridled suburbanization of economic activity dramatically slowed in the early twenty-first century. The historic pivotal points that benchmark the key stages of development of New Jersey are discussed below.

Rural New Jersey: 1790 to 1800

At the beginning of the nineteenth century, New Jersey was a rural society with a marked absence of population centers comparable to the great urban concentrations of Europe. Dispersed rural populations surrounding small towns and villages defined the state's development pattern. The villages and towns were nascent trade centers predicated to a large degree on agricultural and mining (iron) functions, water power for mills and early textile processing, and mercantile activities. The forces leading to their evolution, then, were trade, agricultural, water power and/or transportation requirements (which are the subject of chapter 4). They were situated in reference to the primary shipping modes—water transportation and early road networks—as well as to sources of water power. They were focused on seaports located on the Hudson or Delaware Rivers, or rivers flowing into them. The water-based origins of present-day cities such as Elizabeth, New Brunswick, Newark, Perth Amboy, and Trenton can be traced to their emergence during this period.

Many of the transportation linkages were geared to New York City and Philadelphia, even though the latter were also still in a relatively early state of development. It was during this time that the New York City–Philadelphia axis grew, a corridor within which much of New Jersey's population would reside. Many of the early settlements located there were destined to evolve into the major cities of the Civil War era and would eventually provide the framework for the network of railroads that emerged in midcentury. Thus, the initial foundations of urban–industrial New Jersey were set down during this period.

The Rise of the Industrial City: 1850 to 1870

By 1850, New Jersey began to experience the effects of the emerging industrial era; its physical expression was the rise of the industrial city. The successive developments of the canal and railroad systems and the emergence of steam power became important centralizing forces drawing populations to urban areas—the focal points of the industrial economy. The cities' populations—fed by rural-to-urban and international migrations—massed around emerging factory structures and were dependent on close pedestrian linkages. A tight, dense, interdependent urban complex evolved, with residences closely linked to workplaces, and service facilities clustering near their residential markets. The urban way of life began to secure critical mass in New Jersey. This was the start of the first major economic transformation of the state.

In the decades after the Civil War, the business of the Garden State economy was transformed from strictly growing things to strictly making things. This was part of a broader national transformation. In the second half of the nineteenth century, manufacturing firms agglomerated in urban locations because of rail- and water-based transportation advantages, basic but unique economic infrastructure (roads, water supply, sewers, and energy availability), and ample pools of skilled and unskilled labor.

New Jersey's "big six" cities—Camden, Elizabeth, Jersey City, Newark, Paterson, and Trenton—all thrived and developed in the nineteenth century as urban manufacturing centers. Paterson became known as Silk City USA. "Trenton Makes, the World Takes" and "On Camden Supplies, the World Relies" were not merely slogans but economic reality. New Jersey was a technology-driven, urban manufacturing dynamo by the time the twentieth century arrived and was at the leading edge of global industrialization.

In the last part of the nineteenth century Menlo Park, New Jersey, became home to what could be called one of the nation's first industrial research laboratories. There, Thomas Edison produced a series of seminal innovations, such as the electric light and the phonograph, which transformed the nation and the world and generated enormous new industries as well as millions of jobs.

In the first half of the then new twentieth century, New Jersey could boast proudly of the mammoth Singer Sewing Machine plant in Elizabeth—one of the largest sewing machine manufacturing facilities in the world, which at its peak employed 10,000 workers; the RCA Radio Victor factory in Camden, one of the largest of its type in the world; and Western Electric in Kearny—the world's leading telephone manufacturing complex. All of these businesses, and many others, sold their outputs in national and world markets, bringing large revenue flows back to New Jersey. However, in an economic process of "creative destruction,"[2] by the 1980s all of these businesses were reduced to a historical memory.

Early Metropolitanization: 1920 to 1940

By 1920, a new spatial pattern had emerged: the early industrial metropolis. This evolutionary stage was given impetus by the
growth of electric power systems and the internal combustion
engine. The cities, crowded to the bursting point, spilled their
boundaries and began to encompass adjacent political units. The
city was still the dominant focus of the New Jersey economy, but
a host of contiguous territories became a viable and functional
part of the daily urban system. Residential clusters developed
outside the city but were tightly dependent upon it for most
economic and social functions. Thus, the rise of the metropolis
was a consequence of continued urban importance as well as the
development of outlying suburban residential communities.

The earliest suburbs, which developed at the end of the
nineteenth and the start of the twentieth century, were of a
highly disciplined nature. Constrained by transportation technology, they were intimately tied to streetcar systems and early
commuter rail lines. Hence, suburban development took a clus-
tered form about commuter stations. The spatial spread of suburbs was often limited by feasible walking distances. Perhaps
better described as suburban villages, these suburbs established
the image of suburbia that persists to the present day.

But during the 1920s, suburbanization also became linked to
the growing ownership of the private automobile and the early
development of the state's highway system. From 1920 to 1930
car ownership grew markedly, opening more suburban territory
for development. The automobile overrode the constraining
forces that disciplined the pattern of early suburbs and enabled
growth to spread indiscriminately. Urban and suburban sprawl
was born during this period, although the city was still the central element for the day-to-day activities of most of the state's
urban and suburban populations.

Postwar Suburbanization and the Decline of the City:
1950 to 1970

Urban manufacturing dominated America's economic geography through the end of World War II, with New Jersey being a model example. But the unique advantages of urban locations began to fade as new technologies, infrastructure, and workforces spread to suburban areas in the postwar decades. It was soon discovered that such once-frontier, residential-only territories had business cost and efficiency advantages, and they quickly became the new location of choice as postwar consumption and production boomed. Urban manufacturing then began its long slide, but newer suburban facilities flourished.

The forces of suburbanization, held in check by the Depression and World War II, immediately reasserted themselves at the end of the decade of the 1940s. A population formerly economically constrained by war demanded and was now able to afford new housing, which skyrocketed as a consequence of the high rate of household formation, strong economic growth, and the home-loan provisions of the GI Bill.

This was the era of baby boom–inspired tract-house suburban New Jersey.[3] Approximately one thousand housing units were added to New Jersey's shelter inventory each week—a pace sustained for more than a thousand straight weeks! Thus, New Jersey gained approximately one million housing units over a twenty-year period. The great majority were Levittown-style units filling the suburban jurisdictions of the counties that housed the state's major cities, such as Essex and Union. This vast physical transformation was facilitated by unprecedented levels of automobile ownership, the excellent prewar state highway system, the opening of the state's toll roads, and the initial stages of the Interstate Highway System.[4]

Throughout this period, the New Jersey city increasingly faced a crisis of function: Activities once the sole province of the central city became dispersed throughout the metropolis. Electronics, chemicals and pharmaceuticals, telecommunications, and mass production changed the profile of the state's industrial base. The increasing reliance on trucking, as well as single-story manufacturing structures, rendered obsolete many dimensions of the dense physical structure of urban New Jersey.

The Second Transformation Origins: 1970 to 1980

New Jersey's manufacturing economy peaked in 1969; a sustained hemorrhage of manufacturing jobs and a sustained diminution in relative economic importance then ensued. The old industrial base of the state's cities virtually disappeared after the Vietnam War came to a close.

But a second major technology-driven transformation was just beginning—the emergence of a postindustrial knowledge-dependent, information-age economy. The opening of AT&T's Long Lines complex in Bedminster in 1976 and its global headquarters in Basking Ridge in 1977 quickly became powerful symbols of the state's high-technology future. New Jersey became nothing less than "global telecommunications central." These advanced-stage "teleco" facilities also legitimized once frontier rural sites as market-acceptable geographic locations for office development in New Jersey. Before that time, the region's office market was overwhelmingly centered in Manhattan.

The foundations of the broader postindustrial economy that emerged from the second major economic transformation were set in this decade. And its suburban shift followed the pattern of manufacturing of decades earlier. Occupying the new suburban office inventories in the 1980s and 1990s were technology-dependent professional and business services, financial activities, and information services. These sectors were at the heart of a new economy accompanied by strong employment and income growth, and New Jersey found itself at the leading technological edge of a second global economic reordering. Once again, New Jersey's economy had successfully reinvented itself.

Edge City New Jersey and the Emergence of the Wealth Belt: 1980 to 2000

Suburbanization forces reached a new crescendo in the final decades of the century. The new economy that emerged during this period had several dimensions. Spatially, all of the economic functions once solely the province of the central cities—workplace, residence place, shopping place, health place, cultural place, and recreation place—became dispersed throughout the metropolis. New Jersey changed from a badly aging manufacturing state to a leading-edge information-age service economy, comprising legions of high-wage, middle-skilled knowledge workers. The latter filled the state's burgeoning new office inventory, the factory floors of the new economy.

Emerging out of the 1981–82 national recession was New Jersey's great 1980s office building boom, which completely reinvented and transformed the state's economic landscape. By 1990, North Central New Jersey had emerged as the fifth-largest metropolitan office market in the country, with much of the new inventory located in freeway-oriented suburban growth corridors. The earlier decade of the 1980s had witnessed the construction of 80 percent of all the office space ever built in the history of the state.

Much of this new product, and that subsequently produced in the 1990s, was located in the state's now freeway-oriented, auto-dependent, suburban growth corridors. This became the Garden State's end-of-millennium core economic specialization—its unique nation-leading spatial competency.[5] New Jersey was recognized globally as the leading example of emerging edge cities, supposedly the future shape of the American economy.[6] There was a national buzz about the emerging Route 1 Princeton corridor—the "zip" strip—as well as the I-287 corridor and

others. The suburban highway network became the critical pipeline of the new economy, with the emergent concentration in
the Wealth Belt counties of a new geography for the state.

Another hallmark of this era was the completion of an
enclosed superregional mall grid. New Jersey would ultimately
contain twenty-nine such behemoths before this retail format
ran its course, as it ultimately began to succumb to regional
mall fatigue as the century came to a close.[7] But throughout the
1980s, the new regional mall grid totally dominated New Jersey's
retailing. The state's cities were the clear-cut losers—regional
malls the clear-cut victors—in the retail wars for a growing and
higher-income, higher-spending population. During the 1990s,
the "malling" of New Jersey was replaced by the "big boxing"
and "power centering" of New Jersey, as new retailing formats
proliferated throughout the suburban arena, both supplementing
and competing with the regional mall grid.

The initial economic force in the late 1970s and 1980s was
the emergence of the first-generation postindustrial economy.
Massive growth in service, finance, and other white-collar corporate employment, mostly sheltered in the new suburban office
inventory, defined the decade of the 1980s. While this first-
generation postindustrial economy was not particularly efficient,
principally because productivity advances were hindered by
struggles to successfully incorporate computerization and information technology, its spatial impacts were dramatic.

In the 1990s, the second-generation postindustrial era
emerged—a much more efficient and productive knowledge-
dependent, information-age economy. This era was, and still is,
being driven by globalization, deregulation, sustained innovation,
and the rise to dominance of information technology. Key end-
of-century forces and economic sectors would include semi-
conductors, software, fiber optics, digital networks, the Internet,
genetics, and the new media—completely different from the
steam, rail, and heavy production paradigm that underpinned

the earlier rise of New Jersey's industrial cities. Then, in the twenty-first century, accelerating advancements in information technology and the powerful emergence of a post–baby boom workforce changed the state's economic paradigm even further—a far cry from isolated suburban locations in highway-dependent locations with large concentrations of administrative, monitoring, and reporting service job functions that were the foundations for the shift from manufacturing to the new service economy.

New Jersey versus New York City

Another way of viewing the dramatic changes in the second half of the twentieth century is to compare New Jersey's and New York City's employment trajectories. In 1950, New Jersey's economy—measured by total employment—was less than one-half the size of New York City's, the nation's unquestioned economic epicenter. But over the next fifty years, the region's employment geography was fundamentally reconstituted. By the mid-1980s, the state's employment base gained parity with New York City; by the year 2000 it actually eclipsed it by a substantial margin. At that time, New Jersey's total employment base was 7 percent larger than that of New York City.

In the final three decades of this fifty-year period, the state served as a powerful regional economic locomotive, led by its burgeoning office markets that were largely concentrated in highway-oriented suburban growth corridors.[8] New Jersey became the most efficient and cost-competitive place for doing postindustrial business in the broad metropolitan region. Let's take a more detailed look at the employment shifts during three distinct periods between 1950 and 2000.

1950 TO 1970. In 1950, New York City's total employment (3,468,200 jobs) was slightly more than double that of New Jersey (1,656,800 jobs) (table 3.1).[9] It was the unchallenged

TABLE 3.1

New Jersey and New York City Employment
1950–2013 (nonseasonally adjusted annual averages)

Year	New Jersey	New York City	Ratio: NJ/NYC
1950	1,656,800	3,468,200	0.48
1970	2,606,200	3,745,500	0.70
1980	3,060,400	3,301,700	0.93
1985	3,414,100	3,488,500	0.98
1988	3,651,000	3,605,800	1.01
2000	3,994,500	3,718,600	1.07
2003	3,978,800	3,531,700	1.13
2013	3,907,000	3,996,500	0.98

SOURCE: U.S. Bureau of Labor Statistics.

leader of a centralized regional economy. At that time, America was well into a glorious postwar period of global economic hegemony that would transform the old economic world order. New Jersey benefited greatly from two powerful emerging forces—unfettered residential suburbanization and the parallel development of a robust consumer economy. Vast migrations of New York City's middle-class, child-rearing households to the emerging suburban frontier were fully under way. New Jersey also produced many of the consumer goods that stocked the new suburbs, such as the automobiles, washing machines, refrigerators, telephones, black-and-white tube TVs, and so on that made this new residential geography possible. Between 1950 and 1970, New Jersey added nearly one million (947,499) jobs, while New York City gained just 277,300 jobs, significantly less than one-third.[10] At the same time, the manufacturing sector grew substantially in New Jersey, reaching its all-time peak of 890,000 jobs in 1969—nearly one out of three total jobs in the state.

1970 TO 1980. The decade of the 1970s brought with it significant changes to the nation and region. It turned out to be a period of unanticipated change. Increasing global competition began to challenge America's economic dominance, and two sharp energy shocks redefined the world energy order. The "Rise of the Sunbelt" and the "Decline of the Northeast" were catchphrases capturing new patterns of growth within the United States. New Jersey's and New York City's great manufacturing hemorrhages began. New Jersey, however, still added 454,200 jobs, almost matching the two-decade growth performance of the 1950–70 period (+474,700 jobs per decade). In contrast, New York City experienced a substantial employment decline (-443,800 jobs) between 1970 and 1980 as crime and fiscal crises took their tolls. By 1980, New Jersey's employment level (3,060,400 jobs) was closing in on that of New York City (3,301,700 jobs). So, in thirty years, New Jersey's employment moved from 48 percent (1950) of New York City's to 93 percent (1980). The gap was narrowing substantially.

1980 TO 2000. The 1980–2000 period was one of further decentralization and suburbanization, encompassing all dimensions of the regional economy. In the midst of this reordering, New Jersey had fully evolved from a minor regional participant to a major regional player. By 1988, the state finally surpassed New York City in total employment (3,651,000 jobs versus 3,605,800 jobs). And, by the end of the century (2000), New Jersey's total employment level (3,994,500 jobs) was 7 percent greater than that of New York City (3,718,600 jobs). However, New York City finally began to add jobs following the losses of the 1970s. Between 1980 and 2000, it gained 416,900 jobs. Nonetheless, New Jersey had added 934,100 jobs during the same twenty-year period, more than double that of New York City.

44 CHAPTER 3

ONE-HALF CENTURY
OF SUBURBANIZATION

The remarkable half-century-long metropolitan transformation was striking. During the fifty-year period between 1950 and 2000, New Jersey experienced a total employment increase of 2,337,700 jobs. This was almost ten times the gain achieved by New York City (250,400 jobs) (see table 3.1). Much of this broad economic reordering paralleled the life cycle of the baby boom generation—that vastly oversized population cohort born between 1946 and 1964.[11] To badly paraphrase a popular state slogan from the former governor Thomas Kean era: "The baby boom and New Jersey—perfect together." The baby boom dominated New Jersey, its economy, and its markets throughout each of its life-cycle stages. It lived the good suburban life throughout the second half of the twentieth century. It not only was born, reared, and educated in suburbia, it formed households there, consumed there, worked in the new office inventory there, traded up in the housing market there, and reached the peak of its housing consumption there. However, while the baby boom is still a major economic force, a new demographic emerged to help reshape the economy yet again.

Post-2000

Many of the forces and trends that shaped the second half of the twentieth century began to change in the early years of the twenty-first century. Growth in employment slowed, and its structural composition changed dramatically. At the same time, new demographics began to reshape the workforce, workplace geography, and housing markets. The greatest age-structure transformation in history was well under way by 2011, when the first baby boomer turned sixty-five years of age. In that same year, the echo boom generation—which was born between 1977 and 1995, and was almost the size of the original baby boom—accounted for all of the nation's young adult population under thirty-five years old. New workplace and residence-place values and preferences emerged.

There were also profound advances in information technology during the 2000s—particularly mobile technology—while the forces of globalization started to fundamentally alter knowledge-based work and its accompanying business models. The nature of work changed, how the work was done changed, and where it was done changed. Moreover, suburban office corridors aged, sometimes badly, and were no longer cutting edge.

The New Jersey–New York employment interrelationship also illustrates the new pattern of economic growth in the post-2000 period. New Jersey's employment advantage over New York City peaked in 2003, when the state's job base was 13 percent larger than the city's. This happened just as the 2001–03 national employment downturn ended. During the next ten years, in a reversal of roles, New York City became the regional growth locomotive. Between 2003 and 2013, it was New Jersey that lost employment (-71,800 jobs), while New York City gained (464,800 jobs) (see table 3.1).[12]

As a result, by 2013, New Jersey lost its employment advantage and had 2 percent fewer jobs than New York City. This reversal took the state back to its relative position of 1985, more than a quarter of a century earlier, when the state was still in the midst of its great office-building boom. This economic role reversal suggests a much less suburban-centric economy in the future—an economic scenario that is being played out nationwide.

CHAPTER 4

Transportation and
the Economy

HISTORICALLY, THERE HAVE ALWAYS been strong
linkages between transportation systems and patterns of economic growth in New Jersey. Growth in the colonial era was
spurred by improvements in transportation. The state's earliest
economy was nearly totally dependent on waterborne vessels,
which carried agricultural products from the state's interior to
big-town markets and coastal ports. This was eventually supplemented by new and improved roads. New Jersey, from its
beginnings, was also a corridor state, positioned between New
York City in the Northeast and Philadelphia to the south. Late
in the eighteenth century, the state was described as "a barrel
tapped at both ends, with all the live beer flowing to New York
and Philadelphia."[1] In any case, "New Jersey enjoyed a greater
amount of inter-colonial travel than any other part of America."[2] During the eighteenth and nineteenth centuries, improvements in transportation were linked to further development of
the state's economy, and the state has maintained its role as a key
locus for the movement of people and goods.

Throughout most of the twentieth century, New Jersey had
a nation-leading, highly competitive transportation infrastructure—and a nation-leading economy built upon and supported
by it. The causal linkage between the two was not fully appre-
ciated, however. Now, as the twenty-first century continues to

unfold, the importance of this linkage is again coming to the fore. This chapter details the connectivity between sequential transportation innovations and the economic advances of post–World War II New Jersey. To set the stage for this analysis, a longer-term historical perspective is useful.

A HISTORICAL PERSPECTIVE

Transportation technology was one of the earliest priorities for human development, coming before agriculture and probably right after weapons. The ability to move people, supplies, and materials became the key to human and economic growth, and fundamentally shaped the distribution and location of entire populations. Early overland trade routes, stretching across continents and using animal power—horses, oxen, camels, mules—connected vastly different societies and permitted the growth of commerce and the development of centers of population and economic activity. Water transportation in particular, from human-powered canoes, rafts, and other vessels to ships with fixed sails to sailing ships that could beat into the wind, enabled the economic development of maritime nations throughout the world. Natural harbors, estuaries, and rivers into the interior defined the location of cities and connected hinterland sources of raw materials and natural products to markets and trade. Road building for various types of vehicles, such as coaches, carriages, wagons, and carts pulled by horses and other animals, provided linkages among water-based cities and trading centers. Canal construction and barge transportation, still using animal power, advanced the opening of new areas for commercial development and settlement, and established further connections to natural water bodies and population centers. Canals offered cheap and highly efficient transportation that could reliably move large amounts of material relative to hauling such cargo overland on roads that were all too frequently subject to deterioration and damage.

Then, beginning in the early nineteenth century, and with an increasing rapidity of change in technology, the development of mechanically powered transportation modes had profound effects on the location of people and the rate and scale of economic growth. In Europe and America, the steamship, the railroad, coal-fired (then oil-fueled) ocean-going ships, and the motor vehicle led to ever more economically efficient means of transportation. With these inventions came the ability to transport goods, raw materials, and people in ever larger numbers much more cheaply and faster than the animal-dependent roads and canals and the wind-driven sailing ships that had for centuries been the dominant transportation technologies. The development of powered flight, and, in its current version, the jet engine, provided even further economies in the time and costs of transporting people and some types of cargo. A brief review of these increasingly sophisticated and efficient modes of transportation technologies is informative in understanding the demographic settlement and economic development patterns discussed later in this chapter.

Fixed, smooth, standardized metal rails with steam-driven locomotives transformed the development of the United States and offered to vast areas of the country efficient connections to markets, cities, and major water transportation sources. The railroads also linked the nation's cities and enhanced the capacity of urban areas to offer even further economies of scale with the ensuing additional concentration of commerce, industry, and population. Ships driven by coal-fired engines, first by the iron-screw propeller and then by steam turbine and diesel engines, grew in size and complexity and are now able to carry enormous tonnages of material in standardized containers. The growth of ports connected to railroads and highways led to ever-larger volumes of international trade in goods and materials, and also in the flow of people. Until supplanted by the airplane, the cruise liner had its time of transportation dominance in moving wealthy people across oceans in elegant fashion, and also in transporting large numbers of people in the cramped confines of steerage class. The current vast fleet of supersized oil tankers, themselves fueled by oil, ply the world's oceans distributing oil to fuel the cars, trucks, planes, and other ships that, in turn, move the contents of the world's economies and their peoples.

The internal gasoline-fired combustion engine changed the world in a manner markedly different from that of any other transportation technology. It provided access to cheap, rapid, individual transportation for millions of people. It spawned vast, and increasingly sophisticated, hard-surfaced highway, bridge, and tunnel networks to replace the unpaved, rutted roads of horse- and animal-powered transportation. It affected how people live and defined prevailing culture, led to the dispersal and deconcentration of housing and businesses, profoundly changed land-use patterns, and permitted new locations for economically viable business growth. Truck transportation emerged as the dominant, efficient mode of moving most goods and materials. The motor vehicle also imposed enormous costs in terms of lives lost, injuries, congestion, and air pollution damages on the very same populations that so eagerly and enthusiastically embraced the speed, low cost, instant accessibility, and personal freedom that it provided.

The prevailing historical pattern has been that new transportation technologies emerge, compete, complement, and replace older ones because of cost and scale advantages. These new technologies dramatically affect the location of economic and human activity and determine how we live and how well we live.

NEW JERSEY TRANSPORTATION: THE EARLY PERIOD

The economic imperatives of New Jersey's location have provided powerful, although changing, advantages throughout the years. Positioned on the Atlantic Ocean with deep-water access ports, bounded by the large and navigable Hudson and Delaware Rivers, and located between New York and Philadelphia, New Jersey has benefited enormously because of its geography, its ready access to markets and people, and the mobility bestowed on it by its transportation systems. This was true when it was a colony, dependent on ships and ports and rudimentary roads. It was true when it was a fledgling state in the new American Republic, with its expanding agricultural and trading economy supported by road improvements, steamboats, canals, and early railroad connections. It was true in the post–Civil War era, when industrialization and manufacturing became dominant, and population and urbanization grew rapidly based on numerous railroads with their links to and within the state's cities, to the state's ports, and to New York City. It was true in the late nineteenth and early twentieth centuries, with hints of suburbanization developing along the state's extensive rail lines. Suburbanization accelerated and became the dominant spatial and economic dynamic in the second half of the twentieth century as state highways, toll roads, and the interstate system centrifugally dispersed people and businesses in the new service-oriented, knowledge-based, information-dependent economy.

Road and bridge improvements in New Jersey in the late eighteenth and early nineteenth centuries linked the state's towns and ports and also increased the efficiency of transportation to New York and Philadelphia. Private toll roads, known as "turnpikes," grew in number, quality, and mileage, and, along with improvements in wagons and carriages, reduced travel times and increased the amount of agricultural products, raw materials, and finished goods moving to markets, to ports for shipment abroad, and to other states.[3] Nevertheless, it was the development of canals and railroads that led to the major economic advances of New Jersey in the nineteenth century. The Morris Canal, completed in 1831, connected Phillipsburg on the Delaware River to Newark, and then subsequently to Jersey City on the Hudson River, using a complex lock-and-plane system that covered a 1,674-foot change in elevation across its 102 miles. It was a major engineering accomplishment, and the large and sustained volume of traffic it carried on animal-drawn and steam-powered barges of coal, iron, timber, and various agricultural products was a boon to the villages, towns, and cities throughout the entire region it traversed.

The Delaware and Raritan Canal, conceived and built in the same period, connected Bordentown on the Delaware River with New Brunswick on the headwaters of Raritan Bay. Completed in 1834 and covering forty-four miles with fourteen locks, it became a major route for coal and agricultural products. Pennsylvania coal, transported on New Jersey canals, fueled the growing needs for heating, ship power, and steam transportation in the country and beyond. It also provided the essential fuel for New Jersey's rapidly expanding manufacturing sector. Traffic on both canals peaked in the 1860s, with the volume on each canal frequently exceeding the tonnage on the longer and more famous Erie Canal in New York.

However, as railroads in New Jersey proliferated and offered faster and cheaper transportation of heavy materials, the economic viability of canals declined. Although both of New Jersey's major canals remained in commercial operation into the 1920s and 1930s, railroads rapidly became the dominant mode of commercial and passenger traffic in the years after the Civil War. By the end of the nineteenth century, a large number of railroads densely connected New Jersey's cities and towns. The electrification of some rail lines provided trolley service within cities and to adjacent developing towns.

The railroads supported New Jersey's rapidly growing manufacturing economy and provided the extensive low-cost links for raw materials and finished goods to flow into and from the region and its ports to the rest of the country and the world. The railroads connected the extensive ferry routes from Jersey City and other locations along the Hudson River to New York City. They provided efficient and large-capacity access for New Jersey residents to the expanding and increasingly well-paid financial and professional-sector job base of the city. This transportation infrastructure became the foundation for the development and attractiveness of high-income New Jersey suburbs.

But just as the railroads replaced the canals as the state's dominant transportation mode after the Civil War, they increasingly faced relentless competition from cars and trucks for both passenger and freight traffic in the middle decades of the twentieth century. The focus of transportation shifted from private rail lines to the public construction of highways, bridges, and tunnels, and their connection to the state's towns, cities, ports, and airports.

Throughout all of the profound changes in the state's economy, from its agrarian beginnings to the post–Civil War dominance of manufacturing and then to the service-based information economy of the late twentieth century, the precondition for success at each stage was the support of an effective and efficient transportation system. Transportation was, and is, the key requirement for rapidly, securely, and cheaply moving agricultural products, manufactured goods, raw materials, and basic fuels—coal and then petroleum—and, ultimately, and above all, the workforce that produces everything.

THE POST–WORLD WAR II
TRANSPORTATION–ECONOMIC EXPERIENCE

All of New Jersey's economic and demographic advances of the post–World War II period were predicated on successive major additions to the state's transportation infrastructure—increments of new transportation capacity that preceded and enabled subsequent economic growth. The post–World War II prosperity of the 1940s and 1950s was based on a prewar infrastructure that was one of the finest state highway systems in the country. The economy and demography of the 1960s was then buoyed by the new capacity provided by the state's toll roads. However, it is important to note that the process works in reverse, and the lagging state economy of the 1970s paralleled the lagging pace of transportation-capacity additions or improvements in that decade. Then, the economic advances of the 1980s and 1990s rested upon the new mobility spawned by the completion of the Interstate Highway System, and the creation of NJ Transit. Thus, there have been three massive capacity-enhancing increments of new transportation infrastructure. They, in turn, provided the foundations for each wave of demographic and economic growth—and for the major advances in the state's standard of living—over the last half-century.

Transportation Era 1: The Immediate Postwar
Years—Prosperity Reigned

In 1917, the New Jersey Legislature created the State Highway Department and designated fifteen routes as the state's highway system.[4] Although renumbered and constantly improved, these routes—such as 1/9, 46, 130, and 206—still form the skeletal backbone of today's state highway network. In 1926, the state senate requested a more comprehensive system, and a means of funding it, to cope with growing highway problems. The result, at the time, was the innovative and effective coordination between New Jersey's transportation needs and transportation funding.

Subsequently, in the late 1920s and 1930s, substantial investment was made in the system, and numerous nation-leading highway innovations were instituted, such as the first divided highway and the first cloverleaf interchange. Signature projects of this era include the Pulaski Skyway (Route 1/9) and the Edison Bridge. The Skyway—a designated civil engineering landmark completed in 1932—was a limited-access elevated freeway directly linking the cities of Newark and Jersey City. The Edison

Bridge (Route 9) across the Raritan River was the longest and highest span of its type in the United States when completed in 1939.

The advanced highway infrastructure that New Jersey put in place during this period was the envy of America. When World War II ended and the civilian economy began to explode from the war's pent-up demand, New Jersey's highway system provided the capacity and accessibility to accommodate the growth that would come. Between 1940 and 1960, the state's economy expanded by 703,000 jobs, or by more than 50 percent (table 4.1). The state highway system provided mobility and access for this large increase in workforce and population.

Transportation Era 2: The 1960s and 1970s—Decades of Contrast

As the 1960s commenced, the state highway system exceeded 1,900 miles in length. However, even with substantial upgrading and improvements, it was approaching its capacity limits. The period of strong postwar economic growth through 1960 had been sustained principally on this network. But transportation funding constraints that emerged in the late 1940s and were pervasive in the 1950s greatly hindered any further major expansion of the system. Capacity shortfalls and constraints were about to impact the economy. However, the completion of the state's first two toll roads during the 1950s provided the additional—and significant—transportation increment necessary to accommodate the robust economic growth that would occur during the decade of the 1960s. Just as New Jersey had created a nation-leading state highway system prior to World War II, it then created a series of nation-leading toll roads in its aftermath.

Construction of what is now known as the Garden State Parkway began in 1947. It was planned by the State Highway Department as the State Route 4 Parkway. Because of funding constraints, however, only nineteen miles had been completed by 1952. The legislature ultimately created the New Jersey

Highway Authority in order to finish the route's construction as a toll road and then to operate and maintain it. The Parkway's entire length, 164 miles, was opened in 1955.

Similarly, the New Jersey Turnpike, with the original section fully completed in 1952, was initially planned as a state-long Route 100 superhighway in recognition that Routes 1 and 1/9 would not be able to accommodate the projected economic growth. Again, funding constraints necessitated the reliance on a toll road 142 miles in length. The funding mechanism was another New Jersey first: the largest bond issue at the time—$225 million—to build a toll road.

These bold responses—representing more than 300 miles of new high-speed carrying capacity—facilitated and supported the economic success of the "roaring '60s," which set economic records that still have not been surpassed.[5] As detailed in chapter 2, the forces driving the state's record-long 110–month economic expansion (1961–70) were an accelerating service sector, sustained growth in manufacturing, rapid suburbanization from New York City and Philadelphia, and a potent boost from Vietnam War spending. Employment increased by 29.2 percent, or 589,100 jobs, in the 1960–70 decade, and by 615,000 jobs during the 1961–70 expansion (table 4.1). The New Jersey economic powerhouse of the time appeared unstoppable.

Unfortunately, the boom of the 1960s ultimately succumbed to the "troubled 1970s," and the state's economic powerhouse dimmed. This was a decade when New Jersey's—and the Northeast region's—economic superiority was confronted by a major domestic challenger: a surging Sunbelt that captured increased shares of America's economic and demographic growth.

The Sunbelt's emerging prosperity was based significantly on the new mobility provided by the Interstate Highway System (the Dwight D. Eisenhower System of Interstate and Defense Highways). Prior to the interstate system, the Sunbelt—excluding California—lagged badly in both transportation infrastructure and economic growth. During the 1960s and 1970s, New Jersey trailed in developing its share of the interstate system, with numerous missing links inhibiting its transportation effectiveness. The Sunbelt states, however, recognized the linkage between transportation and economic growth and forged ahead. As a result, new patterns of regional connectivity quickly emerged. The once unique advanced transportation infrastructure of New Jersey, and the efficient accessibility to major economic markets that it provided, was beginning to be challenged, and in numerous cases surpassed, in many parts of the Sunbelt. By homogenizing transportation costs, the interstate system created genuine national domestic markets, rendering southern firms much more cost competitive in serving northeastern markets.

Transportation funding shortfalls throughout the 1970s in New Jersey—worsened by the failure of several transportation bond issues before 1979—and the lack of significant new capacity additions outside of some incomplete interstate segments, had significant and damaging economic repercussions. The state's employment gain in the 1970s slipped to 454,000 jobs, nearly 25 percent below that of the 1960s, and the decade's employment growth rate plummeted to 17.4 percent from the 29.2 percent of the previous decade. At the same time, the newer competitive transportation infrastructure in the Sunbelt was instrumental in its emerging economic prosperity.

Transportation Era 3: The 1980s and 1990s—Two Great Booms

Although the Interstate Highway System was designed in the 1950s, it actually took until the early 1990s before it was fully completed in New Jersey. Stretching more than 415 miles in multilane length in the state, its major and familiar "I-components" today include Routes 78, 80, 95, 195, 280, 287, and 295. Its first substantial impact on the economy was realized during the 1982–89 economic expansion, which set a record employment gain in the state (622,000 jobs). The basic transportation

TABLE 4.1

Employment Growth in New Jersey

Decade Employment Change			New Jersey's Record Expansions	
	Employment Change:			Employment Change
Period	Number	Percentage	Period	
1940–1950	342,800	26.1	February 1961–April 1970	615,000
1950–1960	360,000	21.7	April 1982–March 1989	622,000
1960–1970	589,100	29.2	May 1992–December 2000	578,000
1970–1980	454,100	17.4		
1980–1990	574,800	18.8		
1990–2000	359,400	9.9		

SOURCE: New Jersey Department of Labor.

framework of this expansion was the new mobility and accessibility provided by an interstate system marching toward completion. And the system's final capacity additions were in place just in time to accommodate the economic growth (578,000 jobs) of the subsequent 1992–2000 expansion (table 4.1).

In addition to the interstate system, the creation of NJ Transit in 1979 led to substantial improvements in commuter rail and bus operations as the 1980s advanced. This was pivotal for office development in urban areas such as Newark and the Hudson River waterfront. Moreover, the creation of Hudson River ferry service was also instrumental in the waterfront's redevelopment success. In the absence of commuter service improvements and new ferry systems, office development would have been far less successful in such urban markets.

Based upon the three eras of transportation capacity additions, the reinvention of the state's economy during the second half of the twentieth century was total and complete. A goods-producing economy was transformed into a service-producing society. Moreover, these trends accelerated during the final two decades of the twentieth century.

PUBLIC TRANSPORTATION INFRASTRUCTURE, SERVICE, AND ECONOMIC DEVELOPMENT

Commuter and freight transportation investment/disinvestment has also had significant ramifications for the state and regional economy. Historically, while New Jersey did not have comprehensive *systems*, it did have a *set* of the finest rail/bus services in the nation, with numerous private companies comprehensively serving most of the state and providing reliable and ready access to New York City and Philadelphia. In the first half of the twentieth century, there were two unique features of the New Jersey economy. First, the state served as one of the key epicenters of the nation's manufacturing/industrial economy—the largest in the world. The state's preeminent national role was predicated on the unique concentrations of rail-freight accessibility, which was subsequently supplemented by early highway development. In turn, the enormous rail yards along the Hudson River in New Jersey—along with comprehensive freight lighterage systems—underpinned New York's once-powerful manufacturing sector by providing the means to distribute its products throughout the nation.

Second, New Jersey was, and still is, home to a unique concentration of commuter-driven affluent bedroom communities. The early private rail, ferry, and bus commuter lines to New York City and Philadelphia were the basis for the development of some of the strongest residential markets in the nation. This infrastructure gave New Jersey residents access to a significant share of the highest-paying jobs in the nation, bolstering personal income in the state and creating powerful consumer markets. Similarly, the commuter transportation services provided the economies of New York City and Philadelphia with a potent, well-educated workforce from New Jersey, the absence of which would have substantially limited their economic growth potential.

By the 1960s, money-losing private rail and bus commuter lines began to deteriorate badly. In 1966, a multimodal New Jersey Department of Transportation (NJDOT) supplanted the New Jersey Highway Department. Under its auspices, the Commuter Operating Agency was created to oversee public transit. It distributed subsidies to private rail and bus carriers to support commuter services. But these services, particularly to New York City, deteriorated throughout the 1970s due to both significant funding constraints—three transportation bond issues had failed between 1967 and 1979—and the bankruptcy of the private railroads serving the state and region. This deterioration made New York City a much less desirable place to work and contributed to its sagging economy. Between 1969 and 1979, New York City lost 519,000 jobs, almost 14 percent of its employment base.

NJ Transit, an independent agency within NJDOT, was created in 1979 to confront the deteriorated state of bus and rail commuter systems and to take over the bankrupt rail services. Its goal was not only to repair and expand existing services but also to forge a seamless transit system from the disconnected private bus and rail companies built during the preceding one hundred years. In addition, voters approved a transportation bond issue in 1979. This bond issue included resources for transit rehabilitation. Both events initiated the long process of transit revitalization. The subsequent passage of the Transportation Trust Fund in 1984 provided further funding just as the bond issue's resources were depleted.

New Jersey Transit's improved service certainly contributed to New York City's economic upswings of the 1980s and 1990s. Reversing the sharp decline of the 1970s, New York City added 263,000 jobs in the 1982–89 expansion, and 441,000 jobs in the

1992–2000 expansion. These were primarily knowledge-based service jobs located in a revitalized Manhattan office market that thrived in both expansions.

This improved accessibility to New York City's jobs also fed back into New Jersey's residential real estate markets. The opening of MidTown Direct service in 1996 provides a case example of the economic effects of transportation investment. MidTown Direct, one of NJ Transit's largest capital investment projects, provided rail linkages via the new "Kearny Connection" that enabled trains on the Morris and Essex Line to access the Northeast Corridor directly and to proceed to Pennsylvania Station in Manhattan without transferring. Previously, all trains on the Morris and Essex Line terminated in Hoboken, where midtown commuters would have to transfer to PATH (Port Authority Trans-Hudson). This produced much easier and much shorter commutes for large numbers of commuters and communities.

It also produced higher real estate value increases in those communities having direct access to this new service.[6] The extraordinary positive economic impact of public rail accessibility in the closing years of the twentieth century replicated that of private rail service in the early period of the century, creating higher property values in the affected suburban communities.

Moreover, the impact of MidTown Direct service following the sustained upgrading of NJ Transit helped shift the locational advantage in New York City to midtown Manhattan.[7] The parallel upgrading of the New York Metropolitan Transportation Authority's suburban commuter rail service also contributed to accessibility improvements to Midtown and reinforced this new economic advantage. Even before 9/11, rents and occupancy levels in the Midtown office market far exceeded those of the Lower Manhattan office market.

WAREHOUSE DISTRIBUTION
AND LOGISTICS

Another powerful indication of the linkage between transportation and economic advantage is the state's unique role in logistics and distribution. New Jersey is the third-largest commercial industrial warehouse center in America, trailing only Los Angeles and Chicago. The state now has more than 750 million square feet of warehouse space predicated on a series of transportation/goods-movement assets—Port Newark, the Elizabeth–Port Authority Marine Terminal, Newark Liberty Airport, the New Jersey Turnpike, the interstate system, the state highway network, and extensive freight rail facilities. Distinct economic submarkets are port-driven distribution sectors, regional (New York metro) and superregional (Boston to Washington) functions, and Manhattan/New York City–serving sectors.

The economic linkage extends even further than warehousing. Because of the state's dominant East Coast position in warehousing/distribution, and efficient access to international air travel, New Jersey has become the site of U.S.–based headquarters of foreign corporations that heavily utilize New Jersey's ports and logistical system. Thus, the state's white-collar service sector also reaps benefits from the transportation assets that make New Jersey so attractive to foreign distributors and their headquarters management functions.

PORT INVESTMENT AND
ECONOMIC DEVELOPMENT

The economic impact of transportation-dependent warehousing/distribution functions has been bolstered by the recent resurgence in ship traffic to New Jersey's ports. In relative decline through most of the post–World War II period, marine traffic started to experience explosive growth as the twentieth century came to a close. Trade through New Jersey's ports, once increasingly challenged by other North American seaports, grew at twice the national average since 1998. This resurgence reflected a change in global shipping and the emergence of China as the global factory floor. New supersized "warehouse" ships now sail directly from Asia and provide all-water-route services to the East Coast. This increasingly is replacing the "land bridge," although not yet surpassing it, where goods are unloaded on the West Coast and then shipped to the New Jersey–New York region by rail.

The recent widening of the Panama Canal will again provide a new disrupting force in the competitive national transportation markets by mode and by location. Larger, post-Panamax container ships have to be accommodated. This will necessitate the raising of the Bayonne Bridge.

FERRY SERVICE AND ECONOMIC GROWTH

Until the opening of service of the Hudson and Manhattan Tubes in 1908 and the Pennsylvania Railroad tunnel under the Hudson River in 1910, ferry service provided public transportation links between New Jersey and New York. But by the early 1970s, as bridges and tunnels were built and rail service declined, ferry service between New Jersey and New York completely disappeared. In 1986, NY Waterway began ferry service between Weehawken and Midtown Manhattan. The system then expanded in tandem with the development of "Wall Street West" and the "Hudson River Gold Coast," typified by the new office towers along the New Jersey side of the Hudson River. This development would have been much more limited in scale and location without the provision of ferry service.[8] Today, because of the scale of development along the Gold Coast, Hudson County is the largest Class A office market in New Jersey, surpassing Morris County and Bergen County. Jersey City now has more office space than downtown Pittsburgh.

SUMMARY

Transportation remains what it has always been for New Jersey—a key and vital determinant of the economic success of the state and its residents. Profound structural economic changes have occurred between colonial times and New Jersey's knowledge-based economy of today. These structural changes were enabled and supported by transportation innovations and the availability of adequate investment in infrastructure. Transportation innovations and funding (or the lack thereof) have directly affected the rate of economic growth, the increase in employment and income, the location of economic activity, and the ability of the state's economy to compete within the United States and in global markets. These relationships can be expected only to intensify in the future.

CHAPTER 5

The Wealth Belt

STARTING IN THE 1970S, and then gaining momentum through the balance of the twentieth century, a virtual tidal wave of economic and demographic decentralization engulfed the periphery—or outer edge—of the state's metropolitan region historically centered on New York City. This was suburbanization taken to the next level. Its greatest intensity was reached where New Jersey's suburban rings and suburban edge cities converged. As a result, the critical mass of the state's wealth, purchasing power, and economic wherewithal shifted to what can be called the Central New Jersey "Wealth Belt," a group of counties whose economic and demographic performance was much more aligned with the nation's Sunbelt than with the slow-growth Frostbelt (Northeast region). Hence the Wealth Belt could also be termed New Jersey's Sunbelt—a powerful, cutting-edge, twentieth-century suburban economic agglomeration. In a less-flattering land-use/transportation perspective, this area also represented an unprecedented degree of automobile-dependent sprawl.

However, this new suburban economic juggernaut lost momentum in the post-2000 period. A mature Wealth Belt stopped pulling away from the balance of the broader metropolitan region as suburban allure waned. While still the state's most powerful postindustrial economic and demographic concentration, its relative position has started to slip. The once bedrock assumptions about the spatial preferences of the New Jersey economy have been severely challenged.

DEFINITION AND CONTEXT

As we define it, New Jersey's Wealth Belt comprises six counties: Hunterdon, Mercer, Middlesex, Monmouth, Morris, and Somerset. This broad swath or band of counties spans the narrow midsection (or waist) of central New Jersey between the Atlantic Ocean and the Delaware River, with a northern-edge outcropping defined by Morris County. A series of central arteries form the growth zones in the Wealth Belt. It was in these corridors that the new information-age economy positioned itself—and toward which maturing baby boom housing choices were oriented. These arteries consist of Interstate Route 287, the metropolitan circumferential freeway centered on New York City; Interstate Routes 80 and 78, the major east-west freeways traversing the entire width of the state; the Garden State Parkway, the state's major north-south toll road; and the New Jersey Turnpike, Route 1, and Interstate Route 295 (partially), which define the historic corridor between New York City and Philadelphia. New Jersey was described in chapter 4 as a "barrel tapped at both ends," wedged between the cities of New York and Philadelphia. During the final decades of the last century, the barrel filled rapidly with growing shares of property wealth, income, jobs, and people. The matrix of Wealth Belt growth corridors defined one of the most potent office, housing, and consumer markets of the United States.

While the Wealth Belt defined the crest of the geographic/ economic wave through 2000, the Mature Core Metropolis (comprising Bergen, Essex, Hudson, Passaic, and Union Counties) experienced a relative erosion in its demographic, economic, and wealth positions. But as the new century unfolded, urban decline slowed and in several cases was reversed, while the tidal wave of suburban growth started to ebb.

These changes are revealed by county-based trends in broad
economic market potential (gauged by total population and total
personal income), the scale of individual spending power (measured by per capita personal income), overall economic potency
(determined by total employment), and property wealth (assessed
by total equalized valuation and equalized valuation per capita).
All of these indicators effectively reveal the peak of the suburban
geography of the new economy, and then its gradual retreat.

DYNAMICS

A number of demographic and economic forces and processes converged to yield the New Jersey Wealth Belt. The key
demographic force was the maturing baby boom generation. In
particular, it was this generation's choices and preferences that
underpinned the massive suburbanization of office space during
the great development boom of the 1980s.

As it reproduced itself—generating the baby boom echo—
the baby boom also underpinned the dispersed suburban/
exurban housing market of the 1990s. Large-lot, family-raising,
trade-up, single-family housing dominated a maturing housing
demand equation. The extreme examples of this were the new
McMansions, 5,000-square-feet and larger houses on two-acre
and larger lots, consuming enormous (formerly) greenfield and
farmland acreage. The new "finished machines for living"—the
appropriate label even for more reasonably sized dwellings—
were the shelter of choice for maturing baby boom housing
consumers. The tract houses of the 1950-to-1980 era fell out
of market favor, leading to new residential locations. The new
residential locations of choice were linked to the maturing job-
growth corridors within which the new information-age economy was centered, offering attractive quality-of-life amenities.

The key economic dynamic was the latest reinvention and
retooling of the New Jersey economy. Nationally, the postindustrial service economy completed its full emergence during

the 1980s, with two key imperatives. First, it required a highly educated, highly skilled labor force that is normally found in metropolitan areas. And New Jersey was the most metropolitan of states; it was the only state in America with every county part of a metropolitan area. Second, it required the office inventory to shelter these workers. New Jersey went through one of the greatest office-development waves in history during the 1980s. As discussed in chapter 3, 80 percent of all of the office space ever built in the history of New Jersey was built in the 1980s—the majority constructed in the growth corridors of the Wealth Belt. At the beginning of the 1980s, the state was not a player in the broad regional office market. By 1990, the eleven counties of central-northern New Jersey (which includes the six Wealth Belt and five Mature Core Metropolis counties) comprised the fifth-largest metropolitan office market in the country.

Despite massive overbuilding in the office arena—a harsh reality revealed by the devastating thirty-seven-month-long recession of 1989–92—the new office inventory was available to house the nascent information-age economy of the 1990s. This can be viewed as the second-generation postindustrial economy. It was a much more efficient, knowledge-dependent, information-based economy, where technology investments finally yielded significant productivity gains, and productivity gains in turn yielded strong growth and low unemployment, with strong growth resulting in large income gains—all of which were epicentered in New Jersey's Wealth Belt.

But a new normal, the outlines of which are not yet fully clear, emerged in the 2000s. The great age-structure transformation, advances in information technology, further globalization, suburban fatigue, and changing locational, lifestyle, and work preferences started to weaken the underlying foundations of the Wealth Belt.

DEFINITIONAL FRAMEWORK

New Jersey has been partitioned into six regions for state-wide geographic analysis and for highlighting the Wealth Belt (figure 5.1). These divisions should be viewed as a working set of spatial delineations that attempt to isolate the increasingly complex economic and social reality of the state. Alternative configurations are possible (and do exist), but we believe that this partition is informative in terms of characterizing the economic and demographic forces at work in New Jersey that culminated in the Wealth Belt. The following is a brief elaboration of each region.

Mature Core Metropolis

The Mature Core Metropolis comprises Bergen, Essex, Hudson, Union, and Passaic Counties. This region encompasses the older industrial heartland of New Jersey and its allied suburbs, which experienced the earliest and most explosive suburban growth in the post–World War II years. The region also contains part of the core of the broader metropolitan region centered on Manhattan. It still contains potent economic nodes and zones of extraordinary residential affluence. Its relative share of economic markets eroded in the last decades of the twentieth century, but post-2000 the region's rate of erosion declined and, in terms of several measures, a key Core county (Hudson) began to reverse this loss in share.

Northern Exurban Fringe

The Northern Exurban Fringe includes Sussex and Warren Counties, both bordering the Delaware River in the northwestern corner of the state. Once primarily agricultural, these counties are now highly accessible to the suburban job-growth corridors that matured in the 1980s. Low-density residential use was the most prominent development mode, tied in part to

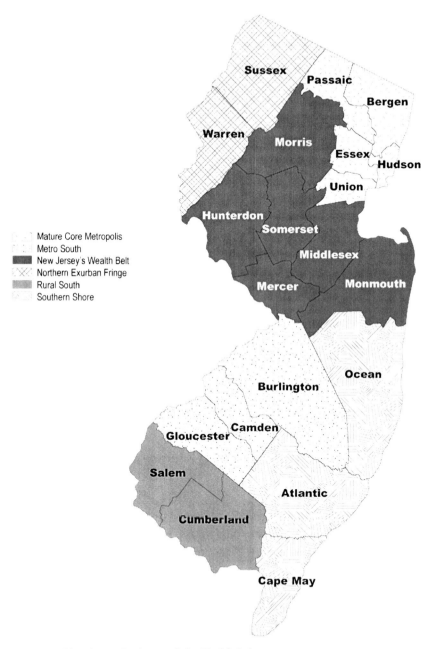

Mature Core Metropolis
Metro South
New Jersey's Wealth Belt
Northern Exurban Fringe
Rural South
Southern Shore

5.1 New Jersey Regions and the Wealth Belt.
SOURCE: Rutgers, The State University of New Jersey.

the economy of the Wealth Belt. However, recent changes once again raise questions about how well the northwestern fringe counties fare as locational choices.

New Jersey Wealth Belt

New Jersey's Wealth Belt emerged with great economic force during the boom years of the 1980s. Hunterdon, Mercer, Middlesex, Monmouth, Morris, and Somerset Counties all hosted one or more highway-centered suburban employment-growth corridors. Generally, these six counties define a key part of the broad suburban perimeter of the metropolitan area centered on Manhattan. Its economic market share has grown dramatically but reached a peak, raising questions about its future path.

Metro South

The Metro South region comprises three counties centered on the city of Camden, once the manufacturing colossus of southern New Jersey—Camden, Burlington, and Gloucester. This region contains a number of early and maturing inlying suburban municipalities, as well as the developing suburban perimeter/edge city of the Camden/Philadelphia–centered metropolitan area. It was home to a number of emerging highway-oriented job-growth corridors.

Southern Shore

The Southern Shore region incorporates within it the three southeastern counties of New Jersey bordering the Atlantic Ocean: Atlantic, Cape May, and Ocean. While the region's land use is heterogeneous—including a mix of bedroom, retirement, resort, and gambling communities—its dominant orientation is the Jersey shore, although the northern sectors are increasingly tied to the jobs of the Wealth Belt.

Rural South

Cumberland and Salem Counties in the southwestern part of the state constitute the Rural South region. This is still a rural, agriculturally focused region falling mostly outside of the commuter sheds of the job-growth areas of New Jersey.

BAROMETERS OF CHANGE

Table 5.1 provides a summary glimpse of the Wealth Belt surge—and then attenuation—compared with the Core Metropolis. The year 1969 is the starting point, when manufacturing in the state peaked and started its long-term hemorrhage. In every measure of absolute size and economic scale—total equalized valuation, total personal income, total employment, and total population—the Wealth Belt's share of statewide totals expanded markedly between 1969 and 2000; correspondingly, shares held by the Core Metropolis eroded significantly during this time. While still the largest regional economy in 2000, the Core Metropolis's once commanding presence is history. But the gap between the two began to narrow through 2012. When individual measures of wealth and affluence are viewed—per capita equalized valuation and per capita personal income—the Wealth Belt also clearly surpassed the Core from 1969 to 2000. But the Wealth Belt's advantage in these metrics also narrowed after 2000. A more detailed evaluation of these transformations follows.

Real Property Wealth: Equalized Valuation

Equalized valuation represents the true, or market, value of real estate property (land and improvements). Thus, it provides a measurable base of real property wealth for geographic areas. Table 5.2 presents the equalized valuation totals for the six regional partitions and their component counties for 1969 and 2000, as well as their relative statewide shares (percentage distribution).

TABLE 5.1
Wealth Belt vs. Mature Core Metropolis: Summary Measures (in percentages)

	Total Equalized Valuation Share of State			Per Capita Equalized Valuation		
	1969	2000	2012	1969	2000	2012
Mature Core Metropolis	50.4	36.6	35.1	104.2	93.5	91.4
New Jersey's Wealth Belt	29.3	36.8	35.7	105.4	118.7	114.2

	Total Personal Income Share of State			Per Capita Personal Income		
	1969	2000	2012	1969	2000	2012
Mature Core Metropolis	51.1	39.6	39.4	105.8	101.1	102.5
New Jersey's Wealth Belt	28.2	36.3	35.5	101.6	117.2	113.4

	Total Payroll Employment Share of State			Total Population Share of State		
	1969	2000	2012	1969	2000	2012
Mature Core Metropolis	54.3	39.5	37.6	48.3	39.2	38.4
New Jersey's Wealth Belt	25.2	35.6	36.5	27.8	31.0	31.3

SOURCE: U.S. Bureau of Economic Analysis.

In 1969, the Mature Core Metropolis accounted for 50.4 percent ($25.1 billion) of New Jersey's total equalized valuation ($49.8 billion), thus indicating the enormous concentration of real property assets in the state's northeastern quadrant closest to New York City. In contrast, New Jersey's Wealth Belt at that time accounted for only 29.3 percent ($14.6 billion).

By 2000, the state's total equalized valuation soared to more than one-half trillion dollars ($584 billion), an almost twelve-fold increase over the thirty-one-year period. However, there was a marked change in its geographic distribution. New Jersey's Wealth Belt ($214.9 billion) just eclipsed the Core Metropolis ($213.7 billion), as both regions commanded a statewide share of approximately 37 percent. While Bergen County maintained its state-leading position ($87.3 billion) in 2000, its statewide valuation share fell from 17.0 percent to 15.0 percent. The Wealth Belt had the next three highest-ranking counties—Morris, Middlesex, and Monmouth—each accounting for about 8.6 percent of total state valuation.

Equally impressive in terms of valuation growth was the Southern Shore region, whose statewide share increased from 7.4 percent in 1969 to 12.9 percent in 2000. This represented the impact of casino gaming, retirement complexes, and resort housing. But it also represented links to the Wealth Belt. Ocean County encompasses many bedroom communities whose residents work in the Wealth Belt, and all three counties provide vacation dwellings for Wealth Belt residents.

Table 5.3 details the post-2000 shifts in the long-term trend of equalized valuation. After reaching its peak valuation share (37.3 percent) in 2003, the Wealth Belt's position started to erode; its share fell to 35.7 percent by 2012. Morris, Hunterdon, and Somerset Counties experienced most of the erosion. Morris County's share fell from 8.6 percent in 2003 to 7.7 percent in 2012. For the same time period, Hunterdon's share fell from 2.1 percent to 1.8 percent, while that of Somerset dropped from 5.4

TABLE 5.2

Equalized Real Property Valuation and Percentage Distribution. New Jersey Regions and Counties, 1969–2000 (in thousands of current dollars)

	1969	2000	Percentage Distribution	
			1969	2000
NEW JERSEY	$49,806,701	$583,827,520	100.0	100.0
MATURE CORE METROPOLIS	25,094,934	213,716,259	50.4	36.6
Essex	5,679,364	41,993,996	11.4	7.2
Hudson	3,125,832	22,902,287	6.3	3.9
Union	4,659,417	35,718,988	9.4	6.1
Bergen	8,467,342	87,293,926	17.0	15.0
Passaic	3,162,979	25,807,063	6.4	4.4
NORTHERN EXURBAN FRINGE	1,104,749	15,863,367	2.2	2.7
Sussex	659,659	9,473,296	1.3	1.6
Warren	445,090	6,390,071	0.9	1.1
NEW JERSEY'S WEALTH BELT	14,572,661	214,946,023	29.3	36.8
Hunterdon	603,600	12,072,273	1.2	2.1
Mercer	1,764,185	21,753,310	3.5	3.7
Middlesex	4,100,573	48,436,430	8.2	8.3
Monmouth	3,105,472	50,550,144	6.2	8.7
Morris	3,313,941	51,479,031	6.7	8.8
Somerset	1,684,890	30,654,834	3.4	5.3
METRO SOUTH	4,529,407	56,466,913	9.1	9.7
Camden	2,186,888	20,747,913	4.4	3.6
Burlington	1,492,120	22,896,055	3.0	3.9
Gloucester	850,399	12,822,944	1.7	2.2

(continued)

TABLE 5.2

Equalized Real Property Valuation and Percentage Distribution. New Jersey Regions and Counties, 1969–2000 (in thousands of current dollars) (continued)

	1969	2000	Percentage Distribution 1969	2000
SOUTHERN SHORE	3,703,839	75,206,953	7.4	12.9
Atlantic	1,094,519	19,644,473	2.2	3.4
Cape May	806,692	17,097,672	1.6	2.9
Ocean	1,802,628	38,464,808	3.6	6.6
RURAL SOUTH	801,111	7,628,006	1.6	1.3
Cumberland	521,422	4,518,657	1.0	0.8
Salem	279,689	3,109,349	0.6	0.5

SOURCE: U.S. Bureau of Economic Analysis.

percent to 4.9 percent. While the Mature Core also lost share, Hudson County led an urban revival. Its share of state equalized value increased from 3.9 percent in 2000 to 4.6 percent in 2012. It is now approaching parity with Somerset.

Equalized Valuation per Capita

The amount of real property valuation per person is another measure revealing affluence and wealth position. In 1969, as shown in table 5.4, the equalized per capita valuation in New Jersey's Wealth Belt ($7,398) was already higher than that of the Mature Core Metropolis ($7,317); the Wealth Belt's valuation was 105.4 percent of that of the state ($7,020), while the Core's was 104.2 percent. By 2000, the valuation per capita in the Wealth Belt ($82,233)—118.8 percent of that of the state ($69,240)—had soared past that of the Core Metropolis ($64,735), which was only 93.5 percent that of the state. By 2000, the Wealth Belt had achieved greater real property wealth on a per capita base than

TABLE 5.3

Share of State Equalized Value by Region and County, 2000, 2003, 2012

	2000(%)	2003(%)	2012(%)
NEW JERSEY	100.0	100.0	100.0
MATURE CORE METROPOLIS	36.6	36.1	35.1
Essex	7.2	7.2	7.1
Hudson	3.9	4.1	4.6
Union	6.1	5.9	5.5
Bergen	15.0	14.6	13.8
Passaic	4.4	4.3	4.1
NORTHERN EXURBAN FRINGE	2.7	2.7	2.5
Sussex	1.6	1.6	1.5
Warren	1.1	1.1	1.0
NEW JERSEY'S WEALTH BELT	36.8	37.3	35.7
Hunterdon	2.1	2.1	1.8
Mercer	3.7	3.7	3.6
Middlesex	8.3	8.2	8.3
Monmouth	8.7	9.3	9.5
Morris	8.8	8.6	7.7
Somerset	5.3	5.4	4.9
METRO SOUTH	9.7	8.8	9.4
Camden	3.6	3.1	3.2
Burlington	3.9	3.8	3.9
Gloucester	2.2	2.0	2.2
SOUTHERN SHORE	12.9	14.1	16.1
Atlantic	3.4	3.3	3.9
Cape May	2.9	3.4	4.0
Ocean	6.6	7.4	8.1
RURAL SOUTH	1.3	1.1	1.2
Cumberland	0.8	0.6	0.7
Salem	0.5	0.4	0.4

SOURCE: U.S. Bureau of Economic Analysis.

TABLE 5.4

Per Capita Equalized Valuation of Local Property and Rank in State:
New Jersey Counties, 1969–2000 (in current dollars)

	1969	2000	County: % of State 1969(%)	County: % of State 2000(%)	Rank in State 1969	Rank in State 2000
NEW JERSEY	$7,020	$69,251	100.0%	100.0%		
MATURE CORE METROPOLIS	7,317	64,735	104.2	93.5		
Essex	6,138	53,006	87.4	76.5	13	15
Hudson	5,112	37,536	72.8	54.2	16	20
Union	8,656	68,280	123.3	98.6	7	9
Bergen	9,474	98,617	135.0	142.4	2	4
Passaic	6,862	52,589	97.7	75.9	11	16
NORTHERN EXURBAN FRINGE	7,458	64,064	106.2	92.5		
Sussex	8,753	65,462	124.7	94.5	6	10
Warren	6,117	62,099	87.1	89.7	14	12
NEW JERSEY'S WEALTH BELT	7,398	82,233	105.4	118.7		
Hunterdon	8,799	98,486	125.3	142.2	5	5
Mercer	5,769	61,893	82.2	89.4	15	13
Middlesex	7,157	64,335	101.9	92.9	9	11
Monmouth	6,886	81,949	98.1	118.3	10	6
Morris	8,801	109,222	125.4	157.7	4	2
Somerset	8,638	102,607	123.0	148.2	8	3
METRO SOUTH	4,848	47,544	69.1	68.7		
Camden	4,848	40,947	69.1	59.1	18	19
Burlington	4,765	53,942	67.9	77.9	19	14
Gloucester	5,000	49,987	71.2	72.2	17	17
SOUTHERN SHORE	8,558	86,485	121.9	124.9		
Atlantic	6,269	77,440	89.3	111.8	12	7
Cape May	13,673	167,110	194.8	241.3	1	1
Ocean	9,049	74,891	128.9	108.1	3	8
RURAL SOUTH	4,448	36,248	63.4	52.3		
Cumberland	4,319	30,894	61.5	44.6	21	21
Salem	4,711	48,450	67.1	70.0	20	18

SOURCE: U.S. Bureau of Economic Analysis.

any other region except for the Southern Shore.[1] It included the second- (Morris), third- (Somerset), fifth- (Hunterdon), and sixth-ranking (Monmouth) counties in the state.[2] While Bergen County ranked fourth—down from second in 1969—there was a decline in the ranking of every county in the Core Metropolis between 1969 and 2000.

Table 5.5 presents the changes in per capita equalized value since 2000. The Wealth Belt's per capita advantage relative to the state fell from 119.7 percent in 2003 to 114.2 percent in 2012. The relative declines experienced by Morris (153.7 percent to 137.2 percent), Somerset (150.8 percent to 131.6 percent), and Hunterdon (139.5 percent to 124.0 percent) are particularly striking. While the Mature Core Metropolis also experienced erosion between 2003 and 2012—from 93.4 percent of that of the state to 91.4 percent—there was a particularly sharp turnaround in Hudson—from 57.2 percent to 63.0 percent. Although the Wealth Belt still has the highest amount of real property wealth on a per capita basis, with the exception of the Southern Shore, its peak advantage appears to have passed.

Total Personal Income

Total personal income—the income received by all persons in an area from all sources—serves as a broad barometer of economic market potency (table 5.6). By the year 2000, New Jersey's Wealth Belt accounted for more than one-third (36.3 percent, or $118.5 billion) of the state's total personal income ($326.0 billion). This income share (36.3 percent) was almost identical to the region's share (36.8 percent; see table 5.3) of total equalized valuation, and the long-term relative trend lines were identical—the gain in Wealth Belt income share and decline in Core Metropolis income share over time mirror that of equalized valuation.

The overall patterns of change of total personal income in each region and county between 1969 and 2000 are also detailed

TABLE 5.5

Per Capita Equalized Value: Percentage of State Level by Region and County, 2000, 2003, 2012

	2000(%)	2003(%)	2012(%)
NEW JERSEY	100.0	100.0	100.0
MATURE CORE METROPOLIS	93.5	93.4	91.4
Essex	76.5	78.4	79.8
Hudson	54.2	57.2	63.0
Union	98.6	96.8	90.4
Bergen	142.4	140.5	133.1
Passaic	75.9	74.0	71.4
NORTHERN EXURBAN FRINGE	92.5	89.4	87.5
Sussex	94.5	91.3	92.8
Warren	89.7	86.7	80.4
NEW JERSEY'S WEALTH BELT	118.7	119.7	114.2
Hunterdon	142.2	139.5	124.0
Mercer	89.4	88.3	86.5
Middlesex	92.9	91.0	89.1
Monmouth	118.3	127.9	133.8
Morris	157.7	153.7	137.2
Somerset	148.2	150.8	131.6
METRO SOUTH	68.7	62.3	66.1
Camden	59.1	52.1	55.5
Burlington	77.9	73.4	76.7
Gloucester	72.2	63.3	68.2
SOUTHERN SHORE	124.9	132.9	149.9
Atlantic	111.8	107.6	127.1
Cape May	241.3	286.6	369.1
Ocean	108.1	116.5	124.3
RURAL SOUTH	52.3	43.1	47.2
Cumberland	44.6	37.0	42.0
Salem	70.0	57.3	59.9

SOURCE: U.S. Bureau of Economic Analysis.

in table 5.6. While the Wealth Belt did not achieve parity with the Core Metropolis by 2000—36.3 percent of total New Jersey personal income versus 39.6 percent, respectively—the gap narrowed significantly from what it was in 1969, when the Core Metropolis's share (51.1 percent) was almost double that (28.2 percent) of the Wealth Belt. Between 1969 and 2000, each of the six counties comprising the Wealth Belt increased their statewide share; each of the five counties comprising the Core Metropolis experienced share decreases. The Wealth Belt was on a trajectory to achieve total personal income parity with the Core Metropolis as the new millennium unfolded.

However, that did not happen. The Core's share of the state's total personal income started to grow, increasing from 38.4 percent in 2003 to 39.4 percent in 2012, while the Wealth Belt's started to slip—35.9 percent to 35.5 percent (table 5.7). Hunterdon County accounted for one-half of the 0.4 percentage decline, as its share fell from 2.1 percent to 1.9 percent. In the Core, it was Hudson County again that led the advance, as its share increased from 5.6 percent to 6.7 percent during this nine-year period.

Per Capita Personal Income

By 2000, New Jersey's Wealth Belt was already preeminent in per capita income, a measure gauging the scale of individual spending power and personal economic capacity in a geographic area (table 5.8). This was a dramatic shift from three decades earlier. In 1969, the per capita income of the Core Metropolis—still the regional leader—was 105.8 percent of the New Jersey average (i.e., 5.8 percent higher). While the Wealth Belt had the second-highest per capita income among the six regions, it was only 101.6 percent of the statewide average (i.e., 1.6 percent higher), and far below that of the Core.

By 2000, these positions were more than fully reversed: the Wealth Belt's $45,322 per capita income was 117.2 percent of the

TABLE 5.6

Total Personal Income by Region and County, 1969 and 2000
(in thousands of current dollars)

	1969	2000	% Distribution 1969(%)	% Distribution 2000(%)
NEW JERSEY	31,930,073	325,986,254	100.0	100.0
MATURE CORE METROPOLIS	16,328,810	129,071,262	51.1	39.6
Essex	4,264,301	29,702,011	13.4	9.1
Hudson	2,378,074	17,811,798	7.4	5.5
Union	2,794,425	20,931,252	8.8	6.4
Bergen	4,873,333	45,564,851	15.3	14.0
Passaic	2,018,677	15,061,350	6.3	4.6
NORTHERN EXURBAN FRINGE	589,665	8,801,812	1.8	2.7
Sussex	311,113	5,409,367	1.0	1.7
Warren	278,552	3,392,445	0.9	1.0
NEW JERSEY'S WEALTH BELT	9,005,347	118,464,400	28.2	36.3
Hunterdon	317,296	6,538,220	1.0	2.0
Mercer	1,342,649	13,966,903	4.2	4.3
Middlesex	2,502,775	27,687,802	7.8	8.5
Monmouth	1,957,696	26,635,776	6.1	8.2
Morris	1,882,315	26,445,131	5.9	8.1
Somerset	1,002,616	17,190,568	3.1	5.3
METRO SOUTH	3,669,300	37,278,384	11.5	11.4
Camden	1,799,148	15,062,477	5.6	4.6
Burlington	1,235,940	14,977,768	3.9	4.6
Gloucester	634,212	7,238,139	2.0	2.2
SOUTHERN SHORE	1,660,285	27,158,944	5.2	8.3
Atlantic	681,323	8,081,534	2.1	2.5
Cape May	225,355	3,327,149	0.7	1.0
Ocean	753,607	15,750,261	2.4	4.8
RURAL SOUTH	676,666	5,211,452	2.1	1.6
Cumberland	438,090	3,427,787	1.4	1.1
Salem	238,576	1,783,665	0.7	0.5

SOURCE: U.S. Bureau of Economic Analysis.

TABLE 5.7

Share of State Personal Income by Region and County,
2000, 2003, 2012

	2000(%)	2003(%)	2012(%)
NEW JERSEY	100.0	100.0	100.0
MATURE CORE METROPOLIS	39.6	38.4	39.4
Essex	9.1	8.9	8.9
Hudson	5.5	5.6	6.7
Union	6.4	6.3	6.0
Bergen	14.0	13.1	13.2
Passaic	4.6	4.6	4.6
NORTHERN EXURBAN FRINGE	2.7	2.8	2.6
Sussex	1.7	1.7	1.6
Warren	1.0	1.1	1.1
NEW JERSEY'S WEALTH BELT	36.3	35.9	35.5
Hunterdon	2.0	2.1	1.9
Mercer	4.3	4.4	4.2
Middlesex	8.5	8.7	8.8
Monmouth	8.2	8.0	7.9
Morris	8.1	7.7	7.6
Somerset	5.3	5.0	5.1
METRO SOUTH	11.4	12.3	12.2
Camden	4.6	5.0	4.8
Burlington	4.6	4.9	4.7
Gloucester	2.2	2.4	2.7
SOUTHERN SHORE	8.3	8.8	8.6
Atlantic	2.5	2.5	2.4
Cape May	1.0	1.1	1.0
Ocean	4.8	5.2	5.1
RURAL SOUTH	1.6	1.7	1.8
Cumberland	1.1	1.1	1.2
Salem	0.5	0.6	0.6

SOURCE: U.S. Bureau of Economic Analysis.

TABLE 5.8

*Per Capita Personal Income by Geographic Location,
1969 and 2000 (in current dollars)*

	1969	2000	County: % of State 1969(%)	2000(%)	Rank in State 1969	2000
NEW JERSEY	4,500	38,667	100.0	100.0		
MATURE CORE METROPOLIS	4,761	39,096	105.8	101.1		
Essex	4,609	37,491	102.4	97.0	6	8
Hudson	3,889	29,193	86.4	75.5	16	18
Union	5,191	40,012	115.4	103.5	2	6
Bergen	5,453	51,475	121.2	133.1	1	4
Passaic	4,379	30,692	97.3	79.4	8	15
NORTHERN EXURBAN FRINGE	3,981	35,546	88.5	91.9		
Sussex	4,128	37,380	91.7	96.7	11	9
Warren	3,828	32,968	85.1	85.3	17	12
NEW JERSEY'S WEALTH BELT	4,571	45,322	101.6	117.2		
Hunterdon	4,625	53,339	102.8	137.9	5	3
Mercer	4,391	39,739	97.6	102.8	7	7
Middlesex	4,368	36,776	97.1	95.1	9	10
Monmouth	4,341	43,180	96.5	111.7	10	5
Morris	4,999	56,108	111.1	145.1	4	2
Somerset	5,140	57,540	114.2	148.8	3	1
METRO SOUTH	3,927	31,387	87.3	81.2		
Camden	3,988	29,726	88.6	76.9	13	17
Burlington	3,947	35,287	87.7	91.3	14	11
Gloucester	3,729	28,216	82.9	73.0	20	19
SOUTHERN SHORE	3,836	31,232	85.2	80.8		
Atlantic	3,902	31,858	86.7	82.4	15	14
Cape May	3,820	32,519	84.9	84.1	18	13
Ocean	3,783	30,666	84.1	79.3	19	16

(continued)

TABLE 5.8

Per Capita Personal Income by Geographic Location, 1969 and 2000
(in current dollars) (continued)

	1969	2000	County: % of State 1969(%)	2000(%)	Rank in State 1969	2000
RURAL SOUTH	3,757	24,765	83.5	64.0		
Cumberland	3,629	23,436	80.6	60.6	21	21
Salem	4,019	27,793	89.3	71.9	12	20

SOURCE: U.S. Bureau of Economic Analysis.

$38,667 statewide average (up from 101.6 percent in 1969), compared with 101.1 percent for the Core Metropolis (down from 105.8 percent in 1969). Four of the six counties of the Wealth Belt had major improvements in their statewide per capita personal income ranking between 1969 and 2000, with Somerset ($57,540, or 148.8 percent of the state average), Morris ($56,108, or 145.1 percent), and Hunterdon ($53,339, or 137.9 percent) ranking first, second, and third in 2000. In contrast, all five counties of the Core Metropolis experienced a loss in statewide rank, with Bergen falling from first to fourth.

Thus, the portrait painted by per capita personal income is essentially similar to that sketched by equalized valuation per capita. It shows a Wealth Belt in 2000 dominating the state and steadily increasing its commanding position in individual economic capacity. However, per capita income also shows the reversals that have taken place since 2000 (table 5.9). Between 2003 and 2012, the per capita income of the Core increased from 99.4 percent of that of the state to 102.5 percent, led by the strong advance of Hudson County (77.8 percent to 91.0 percent). In contrast, the per capita income in the Wealth Belt decreased from 115.4 percent of that of the state to 113.4 percent during the same time period. This relative loss of advantage was led by Hunterdon County. In 2003, its per capita income was 143.5 percent of that of the state, the highest of any county. By

TABLE 5.9

Per Capita Income:
Percentage of State Level by Region and County, 2000, 2003, 2012

	2000(%)	2003(%)	2012(%)
NEW JERSEY	100.0	100.0	100.0
MATURE CORE METROPOLIS	101.1	99.4	102.5
Essex	97.0	96.1	99.8
Hudson	75.5	77.8	91.0
Union	103.5	102.0	97.9
Bergen	133.1	126.1	127.2
Passaic	79.4	80.8	81.7
NORTHERN EXURBAN FRINGE	91.9	92.7	91.3
Sussex	96.7	97.5	94.8
Warren	85.3	86.1	86.5
NEW JERSEY'S WEALTH BELT	117.2	115.4	113.4
Hunterdon	137.9	143.5	131.2
Mercer	102.8	106.6	101.3
Middlesex	95.1	95.9	94.8
Monmouth	111.7	110.0	111.7
Morris	145.1	137.5	134.7
Somerset	148.8	139.3	138.0
METRO SOUTH	81.2	87.1	86.2
Camden	76.9	84.3	82.8
Burlington	91.3	95.4	92.9
Gloucester	73.0	78.4	81.6
SOUTHERN SHORE	80.8	83.5	79.7
Atlantic	82.4	82.4	76.6
Cape May	84.1	90.7	95.1
Ocean	79.3	82.7	78.6
RURAL SOUTH	64.0	69.1	69.6
Cumberland	60.6	66.0	66.5
Salem	71.9	76.2	77.0

SOURCE: U.S. Bureau of Economic Analysis.

2012, it had fallen to 131.2 percent. The Wealth Belt still has a dominant income advantage, but five of its six counties saw that advantage contract.

Total Employment

Total wage and salary employment—the number of jobs located in a geographic area—is a key indicator of the scale of an area's economic base. In 1969, the Wealth Belt's 692,279 jobs represented only a quarter (25.2 percent) of the state's 2.7 million jobs (table 5.10). In contrast, the Mature Core Metropolis's 1.5 million jobs accounted for more than half (54.3 percent)—a share more than double that of the Wealth Belt. Thus, the New Jersey economy was still highly concentrated in the northeastern core region of the state.

By 2000, employment in the Wealth Belt more than doubled. It gained more than 750,000 jobs (to a total of almost 1.5 million) and it increased its statewide share from one-quarter to more than one-third (35.6 percent). At the same time, the Core Metropolis's share fell from 54.3 percent to 39.5 percent, even though it gained more than 100,000 jobs. Five of its six counties experienced a loss of share. However, Bergen County experienced a gain in statewide share—from 11.8 percent to 12.1 percent—the only county in the Core to do so, as it maintained its state-leading employment position. But every county in the Wealth Belt increased its share of the state's total employment base during this period. This surge was led by Middlesex County, whose share went from 7.6 percent to 10.6 percent, and whose ranking went to second place, behind Bergen.

These dramatic shifts came to a virtual end after 2000, as shown in table 5.11.[3] During the entire 2000 to 2012 period, the net change in private-sector employment in the state was -130,000 jobs, with all of the losses occurring after 2007, when the Great Recession began. During the period of decline (2007–12), the Mature Core Metropolis's share of employment started

TABLE 5.10

Wage and Salary Employment by Geographic Location, 1969 and 2000

	1969	2000	Percent Distribution 1969(%)	Percent Distribution 2000(%)
NEW JERSEY	2,745,695	4,100,287	100.0	100.0
MATURE CORE METROPOLIS	1,490,350	1,619,951	54.3	39.5
Essex	444,603	405,023	16.2	9.9
Hudson	269,021	265,423	9.8	6.5
Union	262,738	260,663	9.6	6.4
Bergen	323,184	494,878	11.8	12.1
Passaic	190,804	193,964	6.9	4.7
NORTHERN EXURBAN FRINGE	42,574	77,169	1.6	1.9
Sussex	16,013	39,661	0.6	1.0
Warren	26,561	37,508	1.0	0.9
NEW JERSEY'S WEALTH BELT	692,279	1,458,347	25.2	35.6
Hunterdon	18,834	50,595	0.7	1.2
Mercer	137,704	215,504	5.0	5.3
Middlesex	209,634	432,859	7.6	10.6
Monmouth	136,435	263,149	5.0	6.4
Morris	124,834	304,859	4.5	7.4
Somerset	64,838	191,381	2.4	4.7
METRO SOUTH	313,948	518,147	11.4	12.6
Camden	148,593	220,580	5.4	5.4
Burlington	125,955	202,208	4.6	4.9
Gloucester	39,400	95,359	1.4	2.3
SOUTHERN SHORE	131,449	340,509	4.8	8.3
Atlantic	67,691	153,199	2.5	3.7
Cape May	18,747	43,051	0.7	1.0
Ocean	45,011	144,259	1.6	3.5
RURAL SOUTH	75,095	86,164	2.7	2.1
Cumberland	50,929	62,757	1.9	1.5
Salem	24,166	23,407	0.9	0.6

SOURCE: U.S. Bureau of Economic Analysis.

TABLE 5.11

Share of State Payroll Employment by Region and County,
2000, 2007, 2012

	2000(%)	2007(%)	2012(%)
NEW JERSEY	100.0	100.0	100.0
MATURE CORE METROPOLIS	39.5	37.8	37.6
Essex	9.9	9.4	9.1
Hudson	6.5	6.1	6.3
Union	6.4	6.1	5.9
Bergen	12.1	11.7	11.6
Passaic	4.7	4.5	4.6
NORTHERN EXURBAN FRINGE	1.9	2.0	2.0
Sussex	1.0	1.0	1.0
Warren	0.9	1.0	0.9
NEW JERSEY'S WEALTH BELT	35.6	35.9	36.5
Hunterdon	1.2	1.3	1.3
Mercer	5.3	5.5	6.2
Middlesex	10.6	10.5	10.4
Monmouth	6.4	6.7	6.6
Morris	7.4	7.4	7.4
Somerset	4.7	4.5	4.7
METRO SOUTH	12.6	13.4	13.1
Camden	5.4	5.4	5.2
Burlington	4.9	5.3	5.3
Gloucester	2.3	2.7	2.6
SOUTHERN SHORE	8.3	8.7	8.8
Atlantic	3.7	3.7	3.6
Cape May	1.0	1.1	1.1
Ocean	3.5	3.9	4.0
RURAL SOUTH	2.1	2.2	2.1
Cumberland	1.5	1.6	1.6
Salem	0.6	0.6	0.6

SOURCES: U.S. Bureau of Economic Analysis (2000 and 2007);
U.S. Bureau of Labor Statistics (2012).

to stabilize, declining only from 37.8 percent to 37.6 percent. Similarly, the pre-2000 Wealth Belt's rapidly growing share came to an end, increasing from 35.9 percent to 36.5 percent during a period of statewide employment contraction, with gains in share in Mercer and Somerset Counties.

Population

Table 5.12 details New Jersey's total population shifts by region and county between 1969 and 2000. This was a period of massive sustained suburbanization and exurbanization of the state's populace. Of the state's total population increase—more than 1.3 million persons during this time—nearly one-half (643,938 persons) was captured by the Wealth Belt. By 2000, nearly one of three (31.0 percent) New Jerseyans were Wealth Belt residents, up from 27.8 percent in 1969. Concurrently, the Mature Core Metropolis's share of the state's population fell from nearly half (48.3 percent) to 39.2 percent. The Wealth Belt demonstrated substantial population growth (+32.7 percent) between 1969 and 2000, led by Hunterdon County (+78.7 percent). In contrast, the Core Metropolis exhibited population losses (-3.7 percent), led by Essex County (-14.4 percent).

After 2000, however, all of these patterns of growth tapered off (table 5.13). The Wealth Belt's share of the state's total population barely budged between 2000 and 2012, increasing from 31.0 percent to 31.3 percent. Similarly, the Mature Core's loss of share slowed dramatically. Indicative that the tidal wave of peripheral growth may have ended is the loss of population share of the Northern Exurban Fringe—from 3.0 percent to 2.9 percent between 2003 and 2012. Hunterdon, the fastest-growing Wealth Belt county between 1969 and 2000, lost share between 2003 and 2012 (1.5 percent to 1.4 percent).

The emergence of the Wealth Belt was the culmination of the state's second great economic transformation. It marked the peak of the dispersed suburban postindustrial economy—the

TABLE 5.12
Total Population by Region and County, 1969 and 2000

	1969	2000	Percentage Distribution 1969(%)	Percentage Distribution 2000(%)	Change: 1969–2000 Number	Change: 1969–2000 Percent(%)
NEW JERSEY	7,095,000	8,430,621	100.0	100.0	1,335,621	18.8
MATURE CORE METROPOLIS	3,429,675	3,301,425	48.3	39.2	-128,250	-3.7
Essex	925,274	792,253	13.0	9.4	-133,021	-14.4
Hudson	611,436	610,135	8.6	7.2	-1,301	-0.2
Union	538,294	523,124	7.6	6.2	-15,170	-2.8
Bergen	893,713	885,180	12.6	10.5	-8,533	-1.0
Passaic	460,958	490,733	6.5	5.8	29,775	6.5
NORTHERN EXURBAN FRINGE	148,127	247,616	2.1	2.9	99,489	67.2
Sussex	75,367	144,714	1.1	1.7	69,347	92.0
Warren	72,760	102,902	1.0	1.2	30,142	41.4
NEW JERSEY'S WEALTH BELT	1,969,922	2,613,860	27.8	31.0	643,938	32.7
Hunterdon	68,600	122,579	1.0	1.5	53,979	78.7
Mercer	305,795	351,465	4.3	4.2	45,670	14.9

(continued)

TABLE 5.12

Total Population by Region and County, 1969 and 2000 (continued)

	1969	2000	Percentage Distribution 1969(%)	Percentage Distribution 2000(%)	Change: 1969–2000 Number	Change: 1969–2000 Percent(%)
Middlesex	572,957	752,880	8.1	8.9	179,923	31.4
Monmouth	450,967	616,849	6.4	7.3	165,882	36.8
Morris	376,544	471,326	5.3	5.6	94,782	25.2
Somerset	195,059	298,761	2.7	3.5	103,702	53.2
METRO SOUTH	934,378	1,187,684	13.2	14.1	253,306	27.1
Camden	451,124	506,707	6.4	6.0	55,583	12.3
Burlington	313,161	424,453	4.4	5.0	111,292	35.5
Gloucester	170,093	256,524	2.4	3.0	86,431	50.8
SOUTHERN SHORE	432,812	869,596	6.1	10.3	436,784	100.9
Atlantic	174,603	253,674	2.5	3.0	79,071	45.3
Cape May	58,999	102,314	0.8	1.2	43,315	73.4
Ocean	199,210	513,608	2.8	6.1	314,398	157.8
RURAL SOUTH	180,086	210,440	2.5	2.5	30,354	16.9
Cumberland	120,722	146,263	1.7	1.7	25,541	21.2
Salem	59,364	64,177	0.8	0.8	4,813	8.1

SOURCE: U.S. Bureau of Economic Analysis.

Table 5.13

Share of State Population by Region and County, 2000, 2003, 2012

	2000(%)	2003(%)	2012(%)
New Jersey	100.0	100.0	100.0
Mature Core Metropolis	39.2	38.7	38.4
Essex	9.4	9.2	8.9
Hudson	7.2	7.1	7.4
Union	6.2	6.1	6.1
Bergen	10.5	10.4	10.4
Passaic	5.8	5.8	5.7
Northern Exurban Fringe	2.9	3.0	2.9
Sussex	1.7	1.7	1.7
Warren	1.2	1.3	1.2
New Jersey's Wealth Belt	31.0	31.1	31.3
Hunterdon	1.5	1.5	1.4
Mercer	4.2	4.2	4.2
Middlesex	8.9	9.0	9.3
Monmouth	7.3	7.3	7.1
Morris	5.6	5.6	5.6
Somerset	3.5	3.6	3.7
Metro South	14.1	14.2	14.2
Camden	6.0	5.9	5.8
Burlington	5.0	5.1	5.1
Gloucester	3.0	3.1	3.3
Southern Shore	10.3	10.6	10.7
Atlantic	3.0	3.1	3.1
Cape May	1.2	1.2	1.1
Ocean	6.1	6.3	6.5
Rural South	2.5	2.5	2.5
Cumberland	1.7	1.7	1.8
Salem	0.8	0.7	0.7

Source: U.S. Bureau of Economic Analysis.

end product of a very long trajectory of postwar geographic spread. However, a maturing Wealth Belt may now represent the growth model of the past. It still represents a powerful nexus of the state's economy and demography, but its glorious track record of exceptional growth has come to an end.

CHAPTER 6

Demography, the Economy, and Housing

DEMOGRAPHIC SHIFTS HAVE HAD a sustained impact on the New Jersey economy. In particular, the aftereffects of historic post–World War II age structure variations still stand as "fundamentals of duration."[1] They are the consequence of twentieth-century fluctuations in fertility and birth patterns. The surges and slowdowns in net natural increase (births minus deaths) yielded generations and population cohorts of varying sizes. The conventional labels for these generations are the "post–World War II baby boom," the "great baby bust," and the "baby boom echo." These generations have had, and will continue to have, significant impacts on the economy and on society simply due to their size variations. These impacts become even more potent in the context of changing values and lifestyles, as well as shifts in the economic trajectory of New Jersey and the nation.

THE FABLED BABY BOOM ODYSSEY

The baby boom generation has long been America's demographic tidal wave. Each of its life-cycle stages profoundly influenced every social and economic dimension of New Jersey. It was the primary demographic force shaping the state's economy, built environment, and geography during the second half of the twentieth century.

The baby boom is generally defined as that oversized population cohort born in the high-birth period between 1946 and 1964. It was the largest generation ever produced in American history: 78 million strong nationwide, and 2.8 million strong in New Jersey. The baby boom was the classic pig in the demographic python. To date, there have been three distinct baby boom–driven economic-housing eras in the Garden State.

Era 1

The birthing and child rearing of the baby boom provided the underpinnings for the first post–World War II housing era, which lasted through about 1970. Era 1 can be labeled the "postwar nesting generation" or the "original Levittowners." Immediately after the war, G.I. Joe and Rosie the Riveter married, mated, and nine months later the baby boom erupted, commencing its historic eighteen-year run. The baby boom roared; tract house suburbia emerged. Housing was largely shaped by the requirements of child rearing. The nesting generation and its baby boom offspring transformed not only shelter configurations but housing geography as well. Suburban New Jersey emerged triumphant as baby boomer Hula Hoop brigades overwhelmed its school systems and educational plant. The sheer pace of school construction for an extended period of time was a key economic driver.

The baby boom was the impetus for the greatest housing production period in the state's history, another force of sustained economic growth. As noted in chapter 3, the nesting generation and its baby boom offspring moved into Levittown-style dwellings at the rate of approximately 1,000 per week for 1,000 straight weeks: one million housing units were constructed in twenty years (1950 to 1970).[2] Thus, the great engine of demography drove high-volume standardized family-raising housing production for more than two decades. A vast homogeneous mass middle market resulted. But change was already in the works.

Era 2

The first law of demographics: the baby boom always moves on. It eventually became the Woodstock generation in the second half of the 1960s, inundating our colleges and universities. By the beginning of the 1970s, its critical mass began to enter New Jersey's housing and labor markets directly as young adults and in full force, spawning Era 2. This can be labeled "direct baby boom housing demand." Thus, the second era was powered by the offspring of the first. But the market impact was far different. The mass middle market was supplanted by market segmentation. While the first generation born and raised in suburbia overwhelmingly chose to live where they came of age, new shelter partitions quickly emerged. Apartment, condominium, and townhouse developments sequentially served a baby boom coming-of-age, rapidly pairing, forming households, and nesting. The urbanization of the suburbs commenced in full force as a new, more complex suburban reality replaced the older suburban ideal.

Era 2 itself actually comprised three distinct stages. The first stage, entry-level boomer demand, was symbolized by the wave of garden apartments penetrating deep into and changing the structure of our suburbs. The Garden State seemingly became the Garden Apartment State. A second stage of Era 2 emerged as the baby boom formed the yuppie brigades of the 1980s, and entry-level homeownership quickly followed. Condominium and town house developments then moved to the fore as the emergent shelter format. At the same time, it was white-collar baby boomers filling the new suburban office inventory. A generation born and reared in suburban New Jersey preferred to work there.

A third stage quickly followed, as boomers who had become yuppies now turned into "Grumpies"—Grown-Up Mature Professionals. As serious family raising ensued, the baby boom drove another era of single-family home production that lasted for the balance of the century. It reached its peak in the post-recession

1990s with a burst of McMansion building. Bigger has always been better in the United States, but bigger suddenly got a whole lot bigger.

Thus, maturing baby boom households, in their peak child-rearing stage of the life cycle, continued to reshape the housing market as the new century beckoned. Trade-up, family-raising shelter was in great demand, and a huge web of trade-up markets emerged. Large-scale living and large-scale consumption were the new mantras. Suburbanization continued in New Jersey not only in full force but in full size—big houses, big vehicles, and big commutes. Again, all of these were key economic drivers.

This living large in New Jersey capped one-half century of suburbanization. In fact, the demographics of sprawl prevailed throughout New Jersey during the entire second half of the twentieth century. And, at its core, each housing era of this period was driven by the life-cycle stages of the baby boomers and their housing requirements: birth, childhood, and adolescence (in the suburbs), young adulthood (household formation in the suburbs), and middle age (family raising and trading up in the suburbs). As a new century emerged, a third housing era unfolded, heralding a new nonsuburban-centric spatial reality.

Era 3

The baby boom's national pastime had been postponing middle age. But advanced middle age soon landed with a vengeance on leading-edge members of this generation, yielding Era 3—Maturing Housing Demand and Empty Nesterhood. (In a nod to being politically correct, boomers, objecting to the terms "maturing" and "aging," preferred a new demographic correctness. Their naming preference for this era: "Chronologically Gifted" Housing Demand. The preferred term for the oldest boomers is now "leading-edge boomers.") While midcentury boomers were still living large and driving the housing bubble

of the 2000s, graying, longer-in-the-tooth, leading-edge boomers faced grandparenthood in empty nests surrounded by big,
fast-growing lawns. Thus, empty nesterhood arrived in full force.
Age-restricted, active-adult communities proliferated. As was the
case several times in the past, developers overshot the mark, leav-
ing an overbuilt market.

Until this point, with the exception of a few urban pio-
neers, the baby boom's life-cycle-stage-driven housing demand
remained largely suburban. But many segments of the maturing
baby boom, now no longer child- or time-constrained, desire
residential locations with access to a wide range of activities. The
resulting change in housing demand has opened up a variety of
locational choices. Residences that simultaneously offer walking,
social activities, cultural environments, and access to mass transportation are beginning to command attention. Many locations
with such attributes are found in the older, developed parts of
the state.

The latest signature date for the baby boom generation—one of epic proportions—was January 1, 2011, when the
first boomers (born in 1946) hit the dreaded big "six-five"—
sixty-five years of age. This date marked the start of a vast unfold-
ing of the yuppie elderly market. By 2020, all of the baby boom
will be between fifty-six and seventy-four years of age. Nine
years later, in 2029, every living boomer will be sixty-five or
older. The baby boom's seven-decade-long shaping of housing,
culture, and economics in New Jersey will then have reached its
final stages—and the state will be facing the prospect of a baby
boom-*less* demographic future. But until that time it will remain
a potent force.

The baby boom's final shelter impact has already started to
emerge: the proliferation of continuing-care facilities. Between
2010 and 2020, seniors (sixty-five years of age and over)—
encompassing about one-half of the baby boom generation—
will account for nearly one-half (47 percent) of the nation's total

population growth. They will constitute 59 percent of the growth of the adult population (eighteen years of age and over) during this period. These percentage shares will actually increase in the subsequent decade. Between 2020 and 2030, seniors (sixty-five years of age and over)—encompassing the entire baby boom—will account for more than one-half (54 percent) of the nation's total population growth, and for 66 percent of the growth of the adult population (eighteen years of age and over) during this period. Such shares of future population growth suggest that the baby boom will continue to flex its considerable size and not go out with a whimper.

Other Demographic Dynamics

As the relentless odometer of history continues, the new demographics suggest the evolution of a different, more concentrated, housing and economic geography. Accompanying and reinforcing maturing baby boomers pursuing empty-nester lifestyles are two other less sprawl-intensive demographic forces: the baby boom echo and the foreign-born diversity. In addition, one other cohort will be influential: the baby bust. While somewhat forgotten because it is overshadowed by, and sandwiched between, two much larger generations (the baby boom and baby boom echo), the baby bust will be a force for market shrinkage in traditional trade-up suburban shelter.

The Baby Boom Echo

The first cohort is the direct product of the original baby boom, which started its own family raising in full force in 1977, resulting in a very potent baby boom echo. Before that, the baby boom seemingly totally and absolutely refused to reproduce itself. But then childless couples—"Dinks" (double income, no kids)—were supplanted by "Dewks" (dual employed, with kids). So, after a brief absence, stroller people once again invaded the suburbs, as a new and large generation was produced. This demographic group has been called "echo boomers" or Generation Y—the children of the baby boom—born between 1977 and 1995.[3] They represent the second great population bulge of the twentieth century, and the eighteen-year length of its cohort exactly matches that of its parents (1946–64).

At the end of the twentieth century, America was in the latter stages of the Great Trans-Millennial Economic Expansion.[4] This was a period of affluence and economic optimism, and the future looked extraordinarily bright for Generation Y. Every teenager in America was an echo boomer, and their spending power represented a potent market force.[5] At the time, the generation was labeled "Flyers"—fun-loving youth en route to success. However, the economic reality to come would soon change this destiny.

Currently (2014), every "twenty-something" in the United States is an echo boomer.[6] This is one of the demographic forces underpinning a resurgent entry-level rental housing market.[7] While falling just short of the size of the original baby boom, the baby boom echo is soon destined to outnumber its parents. Echo boomers will then comprise the largest living generation, and with it, the largest housing market target. At present, many echo boomers are living a new kind of extended adolescence— an extended period of pre-adulthood—in part due to the harsh aftereffects of the Great Recession. But most have been in the process of household formation. They are now heavily renters and are a tech-savvy, twenty-four-hour-lifestyle generation, wanting to live in higher-density activity environments. And they don't find one-dimensional office campuses particularly attractive. Basically, they experienced neither the urban decay nor the "bad days" of public transit in the 1970s and 1980s. Thus, their basic life perspectives are quite different from those of their baby boom parents. They have a much more favorable opinion of cities and public transportation. Higher-density living and working closely adjacent to activity environments have gained new market prominence.

The most talented and highly skilled are now known as the "digerati" or "technorati," and they have even stronger work and lifestyle preferences. Such talented individuals that have the technical competency to fill the new creative jobs central to corporate America are already shaping the region's economic geography. Since they are less auto-centric than their parents, transit-challenged employment and distant and dull single-dimension residential locations are at an increasing disadvantage.

THE GREATEST AGE-STRUCTURE TRANSFORMATION IN HISTORY

The simultaneous maturing of both the baby boom and baby boom echo is resulting in what could be labeled the greatest age-structure transformation in history. This will continue to play out for the balance of the decade. At one end of the transformation are mature baby boomers pursuing empty-nester lifestyles, trying to adapt to cutting-edge technologies, and facing retirement; at the other end are young-adult echo boomers or millennials defining a resurgent entry-level rental housing market, and new workplace protocols, location preferences, and lifestyle values. The echo boom is also now at the beginning stages of totally dominating the state's workforce, as it has been entering the labor market in full force, while the baby boom is about to exit the labor market in full force.

The New Foreign-Born Diversity

The second demographic cohort of vast importance consists of the foreign born on a scale and diversity that rival the immigration waves of the early twentieth century. This is adding new dimensions of diversity to New Jersey's demography. Asians have the highest rates of population growth both nationally and in New Jersey, while Latinos account for the largest absolute population-growth increments. The state's economy will increasingly depend not only on echo boomers but also on the foreign born. Many of the foreign-born population are now exhibiting a preference for a wide variety of housing and location choices. During the past decade, immigrants have significantly bolstered housing markets and economies in the state's developed areas and will continue to do so in the years ahead. While there has been considerable suburbanization of some of the more affluent, the largest market segment may not want, or may be economically unable, to make that choice.

The Baby Bust and the Dynamics of Shrinkage

Sandwiched between the baby boom and baby boom echo was a period of plummeting births in the United States and New Jersey. The initial members of the baby boom were not rushing to start families as they came of age in the mid-1960s. The result was the baby bust, that undersized population cohort produced during the low-birth era from 1965 through 1976—the Sesame Street Generation. This group can also be labeled as "after-boomers" or Generation X (Gen Xers). This cohort of contraction—a moving indentation on our age-structure charts—was foreordained to trail in the wake of the baby boom bulge. It has not quite been a demographic death valley, and it has not hollowed out middle-aged America. But it has been a demographic shortfall that has generated pains of contraction as it traversed each of its life-cycle stages. It has had the exact opposite impact of its much larger predecessor—a period of scaling back immediately following vast capacity expansion. For example, in the late 1970s and early 1980s, the baby bust depleted the school-age population, causing overcapacity problems for school systems and educational plants that had finally been sized to earlier peak baby boom demand. School-closing issues quickly supplanted school-expansion bond issues.

Then, as the bust moved into its twenties in the 1990s, all activities and functions predicated on young adults faced contracting markets. Entry-level rental housing demand was in retreat, as the bottom of the housing market pyramid experienced shrinkage for the first time in American history. Subsequently, as the baby bust entered its family-formation years, it represented an undersized pool of homeowner aspirants. During the past decade (2000 to 2010), baby busters caused the 35-to-44-years-of-age sector to decline by approximately 10 percent.[8] They are now fast-forwarding into their peak housing-consumption years. They will cause an equivalent shrinkage in the 45-to-54-years-of-age sector in the current decade (2010 to 2020). These are the ages of peak single-family suburban homeownership. Thus, the population age cohorts that tend to be family raising in the suburbs are now in shrinkage. And this portends a condition of market softness confronting the attempts by the original baby boomers to exit the single-family-unit market in the years ahead.

Demographic Critical Mass

Based on the scale and magnitude of population cohorts, there are currently four key demographic building blocks for housing and the economy in the second decade of the twenty-first century:

- Maturing sixty-somethings: baby boomers pursuing empty-nester lifestyles, resizing in the housing market, and beginning to exit the labor force.
- Twenty- and young thirty-somethings: echo boomers defining a resurgent high-density, entry-level rental housing market, swamping labor markets, and bringing cutting-edge technological skills to the workplace.
- The new foreign-born diversity: with a wide variety of shelter and locational preferences, and increasing workplace presence.
- The baby bust generation: a cohort of contraction shrinking the market for trade-up suburban housing.

Thus, the demographics of today and the immediate future are quite different from those of the suburban-dominated past. They are considerably less sprawl-intensive, and they have already been instrumental in the rebirth of older developed areas. But the full economic and shelter ramifications of age-related dynamics will also be shaped by household/lifestyle choices and economic capacities.

HOUSEHOLD FRAGMENTATION

Household segmentation and life-cycle diversity crosscut all of the preceding demographic dynamics. There has been a transformation in the way in which the nation's population arranges itself into specific household configurations and the lifestyle choices inherent in these arrangements.[9] America has been passing through a profound and long-term household revolution that started and coincided with the coming-of-age of the baby boom. Lifestyle and socioeconomic changes have been powering a furious process of household segmentation, fragmentation, and diversification across the nation. The major dynamic has been twofold. First, there has been the surging growth of single-parent families, one-person households (singles), and unmarried couples. The second dynamic has been complementary: the slow growth and contacting share of traditional married-couple families.

Most dramatic has been the increase in single-person households. At the beginning of the twentieth century, only one of twenty households (5 percent) comprised a lone individual. At the end of the century, close to one of four households (25 percent) consisted of a person living alone. Ten years into the twenty-first century, 26.1 percent were single-person households.[10] This large group of singles has become a much more diverse demographic segment, with the largest subgroup formed by senior women. It is also a market sector growing in economic potency.

The decline in the demographic share of married couples has also been pronounced. In 1960, approximately three-quarters (75 percent) of all households were married couples. But over the next five decades, their share steadily declined. By 2010, married couples made up about half of all households (50.9 percent). Significantly, married couples with children under the age of eighteen—a category representing the classic image of the American family—now account for only 23.0 percent of all households. This is significantly below the share (26.1 percent) held by single-person households. And married couples with children under the age of eighteen actually declined in number between 2000 and 2010.

Consequently, American household preferences point to a future of limited and constrained traditional freestanding single-family home construction. But all this does not mean unconstrained demand for alternative shelter formats. New economic realities have altered the simple translation of housing need to market-capable effective demand.

Demography Meets the New Economy

The above discussion makes a compelling case that there are significant shelter needs that derive from the dynamics of demographic fundamentals. Moreover, these needs differ from the past suburban single-family home shelter type that so dominated New Jersey and the nation in the past. The new relocation preferences of the baby boom generation as it approaches its senior years, the new shelter preferences of echo boomers (linked to new lifestyle choices and new communication and work technologies), and those of a large and diverse foreign-born cohort are all at play. However, the key complementary issue to this demography is whether the expected changes in shelter preferences can be converted into effective market demand and shelter outcomes. That is, will the prevailing economics of the next decade enable the translation of demographically influenced shelter choices into actual housing consumption power? The same is true for overall household consumption, a key economic driver.

A simple examination of income levels within the context of the emerging demography is revealing. Table 6.1 provides estimates of the 2010 median income for various household and family compositions in New Jersey. Statewide, the median household income was $67,681, but this masks large variations across household types. Married-couple families are perched at the top of the income ladder, with a median income of $100,017. This is nearly 50 percent higher than all households. A subset of married-couple families—those with children under the age of eighteen years—have an even higher income: $107,236.

The consumption power of married couples stands in sharp contrast to single-person householders (male and female)—persons living alone. Their median incomes are significantly below the state average ($28,934 for female householders living alone, and $41,040 for male householders living alone). In terms of the economy and broader housing market, income-constrained single-person households account for 26.1 percent of all households, and are fast growing. In contrast, income-leading married couples (with children) account for 23.0 percent of all households, and are slow growing. Also constrained by economics are single-parent families with children under the age of eighteen years. In this single-parent category, the median income of male householders is $45,579, while the median income of female householders is just $27,788. Both of these sectors are growing faster than married couples.

Similar disparities are evident in terms of race and ethnicity (table 6.2). White alone (not Hispanic or Latino) households in New Jersey have a median income of $72,665, considerably higher than that of all households ($67,681). This is a group that is actually contracting in number. In contrast, Hispanic or Latino households now represent 13.6 percent of all New Jersey households,

TABLE 6.1

Median Income by Household and Family Type, New Jersey, 2010

Household/Family Type	Number	Share (%)	Median Income ($)
TOTAL HOUSEHOLDS	3,172,421	100.0	67,681
FAMILIES	2,185,732	68.9	82,427
Married-couple family	1,614,230	50.9	100,017
With own children under 18 yrs.	730,620	23.0	107,236
No own children under 18 yrs.	883,610	27.9	93,021
Other Family	571,502	18.0	44,747
Male householder, no wife present	154,036	4.9	53,556
With own children under 18 yrs.	103,689	3.3	45,579
Female householder, no husband present	417,466	13.2	40,627
With own children under 18 yrs.	375,078	11.8	27,788
NONFAMILY HOUSEHOLDS	986,689	31.1	38,506
Female householder	558,446	17.6	32,183
Living alone	485,451	15.3	28,934
Not living alone	73,015	2.3	73,540
Male householder	428,223	13.5	46,835
Living alone	342,381	10.8	41,040
Not living alone	85,842	2.7	75,589

SOURCE: American Community Survey, U.S. Census Bureau, 2010.

Table 6.2

Median Income by Race/Ethnicity, New Jersey, 2010

Household/Family Type	Number	Share (%)	Median Income ($)
Total Households	3,214,360	100.0	67,681
One race	3,153,789	98.1	—
White	2,340,060	72.8	72,665
Black or African American	428,304	13.3	45,825
Asian	223,319	6.9	94,575
Other	162,106	5.0	N/A
Two or more races	60,571	1.9	56,365
Hispanic or Latino origin (of any race)	436,743	13.6	47,166
White alone, not Hispanic or Latino	2,103,230	65.4	75,974

Sources: Household Counts: 2010 Decennial Census; Median Income: American Community Survey, U.S. Census Bureau, 2010.

and they account for the largest absolute increase in the state's population. However, they also have significantly lower incomes ($47,166). Thus, a number of the major demographic segments in New Jersey (single-person households, single-parent families, and Hispanic/Latino households) are income-constrained as they face shelter choices going forward. In contrast, fast-growing Asian households have the highest median incomes ($94,575) among all racial and ethnic groups. Thus, they represent a lucrative economic and housing market target.

The straightforward arithmetic described above that ages the population cohorts provides a relentless and very predictable time path for the growth and relative sizes of the various generations in both New Jersey and the nation. These future ebbs and flows in the age profile of America are known now. Only the uncertainty of the future levels of international migration (determined, in part, by endogenous economic and policy factors), and the economic capacity to form households, will require that adjustments be made to them. However, while the demography is largely determined, it confronts an economic landscape that is vastly changed and challenging, and one that has profound implications for housing markets.

CHAPTER 7

New Millennium,
New Dynamics

THE REMARKABLE HALF-CENTURY-LONG metro-
politan transformation that took place between 1950 and 2000
was striking in many dimensions. The overwhelming power of
suburbanization during the fifty-year period was vividly illus-
trated by the New Jersey–New York City employment trajectories detailed in chapter 3: New Jersey experienced an employment
increase almost ten times that of New York City (2,337,700 jobs
versus 250,400 jobs). But the post-2000 period has been characterized by significant changes in many of the forces and trends
that produced this growth differential: Overall employment
growth slowed and its structural composition started to change;
new demographics began to reshape the workforce, workplace
geography, and housing markets; profound advances in information technology and the forces of globalization fundamentally
altered the nature of knowledge-based work and its business
models; lifestyle preferences changed; and suburban office corridors matured and approached obsolescence. These changes,
at a minimum, suggest a much less suburban-centric economic
future for New Jersey.

SLOWER GROWTH

National payroll employment statistics were first compiled
in 1939. During the ensuing six decades (through 2000), the rate

of private-sector employment growth per decade in the United States averaged 26.1 percent. However, during the 2000s, an actual employment decline took place (-2.7 percent). This was the first time that the nation ended a decade with fewer jobs than when it started.[1] So, too, for New Jersey: between December 1999 and December 2009, the state lost 155,900 jobs, its first-ever decade loss in employment since job data were systematically recorded. This unprecedented negative performance followed a sixty-year period during which the state had gained, on average, 467,500 jobs per decade.[2]

The first decade of the new century was truly the lost-employment decade. This was also (technically) the case for New York City, although the phenomenon was far more muted. It lost just 7,300 jobs during the decade. The city's lost-employment decade actually took place thirty years earlier in its deeply troubled 1970s, when it lost 443,800 jobs. In any case, New York City's labor markets surprisingly outperformed both New Jersey and the nation in the 2000s. As a result, New Jersey's relative economic position slipped within the broader multistate region, as well as in the nation.

Compositional Changes

The difference between the compositional changes in New Jersey's economy during the first decade of the twenty-first century and the last decade of the twentieth century are remarkable. In the 1990s, the state gained 246,500 private-sector jobs (table 7.1). In the 2000s, it lost 155,900 private-sector jobs. In the 1990s, New Jersey's state and local government employment increased by 24,200 jobs. Thus, there were ten private-sector jobs added for each job gained in state and local government (+246,200 private versus +24,200 public). In the 2000s, the state added 77,500 state and local government jobs, nearly triple the gain of the preceding decade. Thus, for every state and local government job gain in the 2000s, New Jersey lost approximately

TABLE 7.1

New Jersey Employment Change: Jan. 1990–Dec. 1999 vs.
Dec. 1999–Dec. 2009 (numbers in thousands)

Industry	Jan. 1990–Dec. 1999	Dec. 1999–Dec. 2009	Average Annual Pay, 2012
TOTAL NONFARM	257.2	-86.1	$58,644
TOTAL PRIVATE SECTOR	246.5	-155.9	$58,089
GOODS PRODUCING	-135.2	-179.5	$70,036
Mining and Logging	-0.9	-0.7	$31,779
Construction	-9.2	-15.3	$62,369
Manufacturing	-125.1	-163.5	$76,038
PRIVATE SERVICE-PROVIDING	381.7	23.6	$56,448
Trade, Transportation, and Utilities	35.6	-78.4	$48,492
Information	-1.3	-41.7	$93,114
Financial Activities	24.3	-11.0	$97,626
Professional and Business Services	140.7	-11.5	$78,349
Educational and Health Services	130.0	115.1	$48,149
Leisure and Hospitality	33.2	31.5	$22,752
Other Services	19.2	19.6	$33,543
GOVERNMENT	10.7	69.8	$61,731
Federal Government	-13.5	-7.7	$74,271
State Government	3.2	19.8	$66,232
Local Government	21.0	57.7	$58,585

SOURCE: U.S. Bureau of Labor Statistics.

two private-sector jobs (-155,900 private versus +77,500 public). That was not a sustainable pattern of growth.

The goods-producing sector of the economy experienced increasing losses during the 2000s (-179,500 jobs) compared with the 1990s (-135,200 jobs). Thus, the losses were larger even on a smaller total base of goods-producing jobs. Private service–providing employment did manage an increase in the 2000s (+23,600 jobs), but this paled when compared with the 1990s (+381,700 jobs). Within the private service–providing sector, the average annual pay in 2012 was highest in three sectors: information ($93,114), financial activities ($97,626), and professional and business services ($78,349). All three were significantly higher than the overall average annual pay ($58,644) in New Jersey. In the 1990s, these three sectors in total added 163,700 jobs. In the 2000s, their combined losses totaled 64,200 jobs. The jobs that once filled the state's vast suburban office inventory started to erode.

Moreover, in the 1990s, the aggregate employment gains in the high-paying information, financial activities, and professional and business services (+163,700 jobs) sectors more than compensated for the 125,100 jobs lost in the high-paying manufacturing sector, whose annual pay of $76,200 was also significantly above the statewide average. That was not the case in the 2000s, when manufacturing losses increased and total employment in all three of the high-paying service-providing sectors contracted. The four high-paying sectors had a combined employment loss of 227,700 jobs in the 2000s.

The service-providing sectors that did grow in the 2000s essentially matched the growth performance of the 1990s. But all three had below-average annual pay: educational and health services ($48,149), leisure and hospitality ($22,752), and other services ($33,543). Thus, the state's employment/annual pay profile weakened in the 2000s, losing high-paying jobs and gaining low-paying ones.

Regional Employment Shifts

As noted in chapter 3, New Jersey's employment advantage over New York City peaked in 2003, when the state's job base was 13 percent larger than the city's. This happened just as the 2001–03 national employment downturn ended. But during the next ten years, New York City became the regional job-growth locomotive. Between 2003 and 2013, it was New Jersey that lost employment (-71,800 jobs), while New York City gained employment (464,880 jobs).[3] As a result, by 2013, New Jersey lost its employment advantage and had 2 percent fewer jobs than New York City. This reversal took the state back to its relative position of 1985, more than a quarter of a century ago, when it was still in the midst of its great office-building boom. Regional employment dynamics have undergone a profound and fundamental shift.

The Demographic Transformation

A key demographic force has also been instrumental in reshaping New Jersey's metropolitan geography: the greatest age-structure transformation in history. It is defined by the two huge demographic cohorts described in chapter 6: mature baby boomers, many of them empty nesters resizing in the housing market, who represent the workforce of the past; and young-adult echo boomers or millennials, who define the workforce of the future.

For the parents of the baby boom, the new postwar suburbs were an escape from inner-city turmoil, crime, poverty, failing schools, deteriorating public transit, and ever-higher taxes. This parental experience and perspective helped shape the baby boom's basic assumptions about suburbs versus cities. It is no wonder that a suburban-centric vision was front and center at each of the baby boom's life-cycle stages. But even this changed in the 2000s, when an urban turnaround began and accelerated.

Safe, activity-laden, walkable environments are what young, educated, and hyperconnected echo boomers mostly seek in today's urban areas. At the same time, the once tranquil, often pristine postwar suburbs have aged, are much more heavily developed, oversized in residential space, increasingly vehicle congested, and are still highly auto-dependent in an era of ever-higher energy costs.

The suburban allure for many members of the echo boom/millennial generation has waned in favor of edgier urban environments. Hoboken and Jersey City are "in." Western Somerset and Morris Counties are out. A key question is whether there will be a different postmillennial future. As the echo boom ages and fully enters the child-rearing stage of the life cycle, will its love of the city fade? And will the generation change its mind and perceive more family-friendly suburban subdivisions in a more favorable light?

The same shifts are true in working environments and preferences. A tech-savvy generation not only wants to live in higher-density activity environments, it wants to work there too. And these populations generally don't find suburban employment or plain-vanilla office buildings attractive—they certainly don't want to spend their work days in one-dimensional, isolated, auto-centric office campuses. The rigid process-driven office and cubicle forms inhabited by the baby boom of yesteryear are yielding to the open, flexible, collaborative work spaces desired by the echo boomers of today. Baby boomers aspired to "me" spaces in the workplace; their status was often measured by the number of ceiling tiles in their assigned offices. In contrast, echo boomers favor "we" spaces. They care about the quality of interactive team spaces, collaborative spaces, chance interactive spaces—where casual intellectual collisions take place and creative new ideas are often fostered—and choice of work spaces and work places. This is the result of the intersection of generational change and a change in the very nature of white-collar work.

AGING SUBURBAN
OFFICE CORRIDORS AND
CORPORATE URBANISM

The fashionability and attraction of suburban-centric, auto-dependent office corridors may have run its course. This 1980s-based office geography was New Jersey's core economic competency. But new locational preferences centered on a different set of social and physical attributes have gained momentum. This is true not only in New Jersey but nationwide as well. A new era of corporate urbanism appears to be under way, reversing what were once the seemingly immutable forces of decentralization.

The legacy of the state's great 1980s office building boom—comprising at one time a leading-edge, state-of-the-art inventory—by 2014 was an aging and far less competitive product that is between twenty-four and thirty-four years of age. Changing technology has also greatly ratcheted up the internal/backbone office infrastructure requirements—fiber, power, and air conditioning—to an extent that could not have been imagined when the earliest inventory was set in place. As the balance of the current decade proceeds, the supply of obsolete and underperforming office product is destined to grow. The same reality may confront these structures' campus settings and their dispersed suburban corridor locations.

One example is the million-square-foot global headquarters palace of Merck, which opened in 1992. It is located in the western portion of the Route I-78 corridor, situated on more than 500 acres in Whitehouse Station in Hunterdon County. As a result of its merger with Schering-Plough, it will vacate this building in 2015 and consolidate its real estate footprint in Schering-Plough's former headquarters building in Kenilworth, Union County.

This does not mean that the state's outer growth corridors will become echo boomer–free zones in the future, nor will the suburban knowledge-based economy fade away. But it strongly suggests that slow growth and geographic consolidation will define the immediate future. Several examples of geographic consolidation around Morristown are presented later in this chapter.

INFORMATION TECHNOLOGY AND GLOBALIZATION

Office obsolescence is not determined solely by age but also by changing economic functions. As noted in chapter 3, New Jersey's successful structural transformation to a knowledge-based, information-age economy was based on legions of middle-skilled knowledge workers flourishing in suburban work environments. Through much of the 1980s and deep into the 1990s, much of their day-to-day tasks involved pre-Internet information processing and record keeping following routine, segmented, standardized work procedures. This was done most efficiently by having large office floor plates to accommodate such processes, making old urban office structures, which generally had much smaller floor plates, functionally obsolete.

But advances in information technology ultimately kept redefining the very nature of knowledge-based work, and redefined the very nature of the office building itself. Many of the basic work processes that helped define the internal structure of the state's original suburban office inventory have disappeared. Basic process management is no longer the primary function taking place in office buildings. Many of the jobs associated with such functions have been automated or globally outsourced. Increasingly, sophisticated creative work is the new task taking place in office buildings.

Thus, the number of middle-skilled office jobs that were a staple of the 1980s and 1990s started to stagnate post-2000. They have succumbed to the new reality defined by globalization, cost discipline, and information technology. And, as a result, this change is lessening basic corporate space requirements.

In addition, a new era of mobile information technology is, despite its already profound impacts, still in its early years. Already, it is providing ubiquitous connectivity, unshackling and untethering workers from fixed-in-place information technology systems. Essentially, information-age umbilical cords are being severed by sustained advances in communications technology. Workers now have threshold increases in mobility and are no longer geographic prisoners—no longer cubicle captives. A new mantra has emerged: any space is a workplace. This has redefined and extended the spatial boundaries and composition of the traditional workplace. And it has further reduced corporate space needs.

The broader economy is also being reshaped by advances in artificial intelligence, machine learning, and natural user interfaces, such as voice recognition. This is further redefining knowledge-based work, making it possible to automate many processes and protocols that heretofore were regarded as impossible or impractical for machines to perform.[4]

Data Centers: Digital Universe

In a more positive development, data centers are an emerging critical infrastructure component of information technology and globalization. New Jersey is already considered the center of the digital universe—one of the largest data center markets in the country.[5] Data centers are the physical structures that house the large groups of networked computer servers typically used by corporations and organizations for the remote storage, processing, management, exchange, or distribution/dissemination of large amounts of data and information. Data centers are often invisible on the landscape because of security concerns, usually identified only by the street number on the structure. For example, Goldman Sachs's 275,000-square-foot data center on Route 202 in Bridgewater does not draw attention to itself, looking like a warehouse with a fence around it. But data centers are a crucial infrastructure component of the information-age economy, a vital necessity for basic business processes and business continuity requirements. Geography is again proving to be destiny, with New Jersey's location vis-à-vis New York City a critical spatial factor: a major data center "crescent" in North Central New Jersey arching around Manhattan has been developing. Again, early on, New Jersey is in a nation-leading position.

Distribution

Another digital-related economic sector that is bolstered by a resurgent New York City centers on distribution (warehousing and logistics). This has been one of the state's historic economic specializations. E-commerce has emerged as a major force, and New Jersey is strategically located for online shopping fulfillment and distribution for the broader region. Amazon is about to open a major one-million-square-foot facility in Robbinsville (Mercer County) near New Jersey Turnpike exit 7A, about sixty miles south of Manhattan. Closer in, Peapod, the country's leading online Internet grocer, will lease 345,000 square feet in the new 880,000-square-foot Pulaski Distribution Center in Jersey City. These are not the warehouses of old. They are sophisticated structures whose internal processes are highly automated and driven by sophisticated information technology. Many more are or will be in the development pipeline. The state's geographic advantage in an e-commerce era is not going to fade away anytime soon.

THE GREAT RECESSION

The bursting of the housing and credit bubbles of the 2000s spawned the Great Recession and its aftermath. Its severity, detailed in chapter 2, put New Jersey in a deep employment hole and, instead of blocking experimentation, actually sped it up. Thus, it greatly accelerated change in corporate America— faster adoption of technology; redefining basic business models; simplifying the organization to be more agile in a complex, fast-changing world; and reinventing the very way knowledge-based economic activity is carried out. There is a greater corporate recognition that profit comes from innovation. Old-line organizations are the enemy of innovation. So too are old-line office configurations.

The Great Space Deleveraging: The New Normal

Great Recession–inspired and globalization-required cost cutting has finally gotten around to office space utilization. It is now being implemented and maximized. The great majority of companies relocating to new office space consume less space—between one-quarter and one-third less space, as described in the BASF and Realogy examples below. The old twentieth-century question was, how much additional space will we need in the future? The new twenty-first-century question is, how do we reduce our real estate footprint?

A survey by CoreNet Global indicates that average office space per worker globally dropped to 150 square feet in 2013 from 225 square feet in 2010 (a decline of a third in three years). While this trend eventually will slow, the economic reality of today and tomorrow increasingly suggests there may be too much office product in suburban New Jersey, particularly older, outer-suburban product. Suburban locational differentiation is also now becoming paramount. Singular, auto-centric, dispersed and isolated suburban office buildings are last century's model. Suburban product, closer to a metropolitan center, or near to desirable suburban multifunctional activity nodes that have rail accessibility, has much greater future potential: in other words, an urban vibe in a suburban setting.

For example, Morristown in Morris County has been labeled "Hoboken West," an activity-laden, rail-access, echo boom haven. Other examples of recent successful office projects are in geographic propinquity. For example, in 1994 BASF (the giant German chemical company) opened a 950,000-square-foot

U.S. corporate headquarters structure in Mount Olive along I-80 in western Morris County. In 2012, it moved to a new 325,000-square-foot structure in Florham Park, close to Morristown, in eastern Morris County. The physically impressive Mount Olive property sits vacant, with dwindling potential for reuse as an office building.

Similarly, in 2013 real estate giant Realogy—which owns real estate firms Century 21, Coldwell Banker, and ERA—moved eastward in Morris County from an obsolete 370,000-square-foot headquarters office building in Parsippany located along Route 10 to a new 285,000-square-foot headquarters in Madison, again close to Morristown.[6] A third project in Morristown's orbit is Bayer HealthCare's East Coast headquarters on a repurposed campus in Hanover that was once the site of an Alcatel-Lucent complex that comprised 1.5 million square feet of functionally obsolete structures. Two of these structures, totaling 450,000 square feet, were revitalized and incorporated into the final 675,000-square-foot headquarters building.[7] The project consolidated operations from a number of different locations to a single site.

Another example of consolidation and repurposing of an obsolete structure involves Novo Nordisk, the Danish pharmaceutical company. It had been spread out in four locations in Plainsboro in the Route 1 Princeton corridor and wanted to consolidate. Nearby, on Scudders Mill Road, was a vacant 731,000-square-foot office structure built in 1984 by Merrill Lynch. The building was stripped to the frame and reconfigured for the new work environment. Novo Nordisk moved there in 2013, occupying 500,000 square feet. This is a prime example of reimagining and retrofitting a suburban "dinosaur" that is close to a suburban activity center—Princeton—and to affordable echo boomer–friendly rental housing in Plainsboro.

Changing Corporate Strategies

As a result of the forces detailed above, corporate cultures, business models, and knowledge-based jobs have been radically transformed. The new geographic preferences are defined by such attributes as diversity, sustainability, rail accessibility, and walkability. In addition to locational preferences, interior office ecosystems, driven by technology and changing work tasks and work protocols, are also shifting, helping make obsolete the internal structure of a significant portion of the state's aging office inventory. The new work configurations—in addition to tele-working—further reduce office square-footage requirements.

A SUMMARY OF THE
EMERGING DYNAMICS

The future of New Jersey's knowledge-based economy will heavily depend on the future of its massive suburban office inventory. The following summarization reiterates some of the major forces that are now shaping its destiny.

- The fashionability and attraction of suburban-centric, auto-dependent office corridors may have run its course. This 1980s-based office geography had evolved into New Jersey's core economic competency. New locational preferences centered on a different set of social and physical attributes have gained momentum.
- The legacy of the state's great 1980s office building boom—comprising at one time a leading-edge, national state-of-the-art inventory—is now an aging and far less competitive product between two and three decades of age. And it is centered on an aging highway infrastructure facing significant capital needs and a higher energy-price future.

- As the balance of the decade proceeds, the supply of obsolete and underperforming office product is destined to grow. The same reality may confront these structures' spacious campus settings.

- New Jersey's structural transformation to a knowledge-based, information-age economy proceeded in lockstep with the emergence of powerful suburban growth corridors. The state's nation-leading specialization was based on legions of high-wage, middle-skilled knowledge workers flourishing in suburban work environments.

- However, the high-wage, middle-skilled knowledge worker, while not about to become an endangered species, is no longer at the leading edge of growth. This model has succumbed to the new reality defined by globalization, cost discipline, and powerful and mobile information technology.

- Most high-wage jobs going forward will be high-skilled, highly educated ones, and some of those jobs may be only middle wage. The lifestyle and workplace preferences of the talented individuals that have the technical competency to fill those jobs will shape future economic geographies. These preferences have already started to assert themselves.

- Similarly, corporate cultures and business models have been radically transformed. Sterile, insular corporate communities are out. Exciting, interactive, multifunctional twenty-four-hour environments are in, as are such attributes as diversity, sustainability, and walkability.

- Consequently, office ecosystems are changing. The cubicle forms inhabited by the baby boom of yesteryear may be yielding to the flexible collaborative spaces desired by the echo boom of today.

- Information-age umbilical cords are being severed by sustained advances in communications technology. Echo boomers are untethered from fixed-in-place information-technology systems.

- Have these twenty-first-century shifts rendered obsolete the old geographic order—the location preferences of choice of the late twentieth century—as well as individual structures? The lagging pace of employment growth in New Jersey relative to New York City suggests that this is a major issue.

- Other dynamics are also at work. In the era of the great industrial research laboratory, New Jersey stood at the top of the pecking order—stood as a true high-tech capital. Bell Labs in Holmdel, Exxon-Mobil Research in Florham Park, Sarnoff Lab in Princeton, and numerous pharmaceutical research complexes on stand-alone facilities set in suburban corporate campuses were globally preeminent.

- This is no longer the case. The Bell Laboratories division (later known as Lucent and then Alcatel-Lucent) of Bell Telephone (later known as AT&T) constructed a 472-acre research campus (Bell Labs) in Holmdel in 1962. Its final size reached two million square feet and employed more than 6,000 researchers and engineers. It closed in 2006. The Esso Research and Engineering Company (later Exxon, then Exxon Mobil) opened a vast suburban research campus in Florham Park in 1959, ultimately employing 2,300 employees in the early 1980s. It closed in 2000.

- New high-tech clusters have emerged nationally and globally. For example, urban locations that have university concentrations of research excellence with large small-business agglomerations of related tech and life science firms, such as Cambridge-Boston, have become preeminent for the new leading-edge research centers

of pharma and life-science companies. This has nega-
tively affected New Jersey.

- For example, Sanofi-Aventis, the French pharmaceutical giant, vacated its 110-acre R&D campus, which
comprised 1.2 million square feet of structures and
facilities in Bridgewater, in 2012. It moved to the Cambridge-Boston area to be near its biotechnology sub-
sidiary, Genzyme, and to be near academic institutions
relevant to the changing nature of its research activities.

- Similarly, in 2013 Swiss drugmaker Roche shuttered its
forty-building, 119-acre Nutley campus that had been
its U.S. headquarters and clinical research center, once
employing 10,000 people. It relocated to south San
Francisco, the home of its giant biotechnology company, Genentech.

- Concurrently, Manhattan is becoming an emerging
high-tech center at the same time that its financial sector faces an uncertain future. New corporate giants,
such as Google, have made Manhattan an edgy, urban
research destination favored by large and small tech
firms and their young high-tech workforce.

- In 2010, Google bought the former Port Authority
multiuse building—111 Eighth Avenue—in the Chel-
sea neighborhood of Manhattan. It is a prototypical
edgy workplace. Opened in 1932 as Union Inland Terminal and used for shipping, warehousing, and manufacturing, it occupies an entire block and is currently
the city's third-largest building (2.9 million square feet).
It sits astride a major underground fiber optic highway.
In addition to Google, it has other digital-age tenants.
Google now has approximately 3,000 workers employed
there and elsewhere in New York City.

- Manhattan has also become a favored residential investment of choice for the global elite, whose servicing

and spending, enhanced by a weak dollar, now cas-
cade through the New York City economy. Foreign
tourists have also made Manhattan a preeminent destination of choice, with attendant positive employment
implications.

THE FUTURE

Determining New Jersey's future economy is obviously
fraught with uncertainty. Nonetheless, there are two key deter-
minants, among others. The first is linked to emerging national
and global growth locomotives—the industrial sectors that will
drive the economy of the future. Although these sectors will
probably be high-technology, knowledge-based activities, their
exact shape and scope are difficult to discern. This is not unusual.
For example, in 1992, there were very few who predicted that the
Internet would be a growth locomotive in the second half of the
decade and would transform the world economy. In fact, most
forecasters at that time had only rudimentary knowledge about
the information superhighway. But as the twentieth century
came to a close the Internet was quickly reshaping the American and global economy. And it also was directly contributing
to changing dimensions of knowledge-based workplace location
and configuration, leading to the second determinant. Offices
are the factory floors of the new knowledge-based economy.
The ability of New Jersey's current office inventory to adapt to
a changing economic world will also be instrumental in determining the future competitiveness of the state. This leads to the
following questions:

- What can New Jersey do with its vast inventory of past
  physical investments? Wholesale abandonment is really
  not a viable option, but the potential of empty remnants
  of once-viable office parks—the postindustrial analogues
  of abandoned industrial factory complexes—cannot be

discounted. Can some of them be retooled for emerging economic imperatives?

- Fortunately, there are still suburban office environments that are spatially well positioned relative to population concentrations, urban-type amenities, and accessibility. How do we reimagine such existing assets? Can there be a fundamental reinventing of the inlying suburban office campus?
- What are the acceptable models for maximizing a sustainable environment by effective reuse and redesign? What will comprise the successful new campus aesthetic and functionality?
- Office buildings sunk in seas of asphalt need to be reimagined. They will not constitute a competitive work environment going forward. What are the outlines of such a reimaging?
- What other strategic modifications are necessary to create a multiuse, interactive, accessible sense of place? What can be done to have highly talented, highly skilled echo boomer knowledge workers find this an acceptable workplace?

Answers to these questions will prove critical in determining the future of New Jersey's information-age economy.

Notes

Chapter 1 — Introduction and Overview

1. The goods-producing sector of the economy is dominated by manufacturing and construction. See the Bureau of Labor Statistics for a complete listing of industry classifications. http://bls.gov/iag/tgs/iag_index_naics.htm.

2. Data centers, housed in warehouse-type structures, are also emerging as a major economic concentration in New Jersey, although their employment levels are modest.

3. In this book, the terms "echo boomers" and "millennials" are used interchangeably although their precise delineations vary. There is general agreement that the baby boom echo (also termed Generation Y) was born between 1977 and 1995. There is less of a consensus on millennials, with estimates from the early 1980s to the early 2000s.

4. New Jersey was ranked third by the U.S. Census Bureau among the fifty states in the percentage of the population foreign born in 2012.

Chapter 2 — The Structure of the New Jersey Economy and the Business Cycle

1. The website of the National Bureau of Economic Research (nber.org) provides extensive information on the definition of a recession and how beginning and end points are determined.

2. Gross domestic product data is not available quarterly by state. It is available annually only, and with a lag. Thus, quarterly employment and income data are key metrics used for cyclical analyses of state economic performance.

3. As will be pointed out, employment continued to decline in the United States through February 2010, eight months after the technical end of the recession.

4. New Jersey's date is placed in parentheses if different from that of the nation.
5. It should be stressed that private-sector employment is used in this analysis; table 2.1, which defined recessions and expansions, used total employment.
6. As shown in table 2.1, the recession started in November 1973 and ended in March 1975. It lasted sixteen months.
7. This downturn also lasted sixteen months, starting in July 1981 and ending in November 1982. However, it may have been part of what had been termed at the time a broader "rolling recession." There was a brief immediate post-oil-shock recession (January 1980–July 1980), followed by a twelve-month period of minimal, halting economic growth before the economy tumbled into a deep recession in July 1981.
8. The recovery was given a powerful boost by the Economic Recovery Tax Act of 1981 (ERTA), a federal law that, among many provisions, reduced individual income tax rates and accelerated depreciation deductions. The latter had a major positive impact on commercial construction, particularly office buildings.
9. The expansion lasted ninety-two months (November 1982–July 1990). At that time, only the February 1961–December 1969 expansion was longer (106 months), but that was aided by the long Vietnam War.
10. This recession lasted only eight months (July 1990–March 1991).
11. It started in March 1991 and ended in March 2001.
12. Total private-sector employment increased from 72,806,000 jobs in November 1982 to 111,796,000 jobs in March 2001.
13. Technically, the recession (March 2001–November 2001) was relatively brief (eight months), but employment declines continued throughout 2002 and the first part of 2003. This was not simply jobless economic growth but job-loss economic growth.
14. It started in December 2007 and ended in June 2009. However, employment losses continued for another eight months through February 2010.
15. As pointed out earlier, the 1973–75 recession was also sixteen months long.
16. As shown in table 2.1, the recession started in September 1981 and ended in April 1982.
17. This was spurred by ERTA, noted earlier, which produced a bicoastal real estate frenzy.
18. The Y2K problem, or year 2000 problem, stemmed from the inability of then extant software and hardware to recognize the change in century date. Massive amounts of data had been stored listing only the last two digits of the year, e.g., listing 1990 as simply 90. So, when 1999 changed to 2000, systems as then structured would not know whether it was 2000 or 1900, since only the last

two digits were listed. Massive hardware, software, and database upgrades—as well as extensive IT staff expansions—were required to forestall anticipated problems. The century turned without a technological Armageddon, and the previous overinvestment in technology reduced new-technology sales and staffing significantly going forward.

19. This was due to the aftershocks of the state's real estate frenzy during the 1980s, which was far more extreme than that of the nation.

20. Local government includes municipal, county, and educational employment.

CHAPTER 3   THE BROAD HISTORICAL EVOLUTION

1. Multiple dimensions of suburbanization have occurred simultaneously in New Jersey. Within the state, there were outward flows from older urban centers, such as Camden and Newark, into the surrounding territories. Superimposed on this pattern were the outward flows from New York City and Philadelphia into suburban New Jersey. Moreover, while there is a flow of international immigrant groups into New Jersey's urban areas, as well as into New York City and Philadelphia, suburban New Jersey has also become a direct destination for new foreign-born immigrants. Thus, the overall process of suburbanization in New Jersey is a complex one.

2. A phrase made famous by the Austrian economist Joseph Schumpeter that succinctly captures the effects of fundamental innovations on economic organization and structure.

3. The demographic–economic linkages are examined in chapter 6. The baby boom was the huge population cohort born between 1946 and 1964. It was the most powerful demographic event during the second half of the twentieth century.

4. Chapter 4 details the state's transportation history and the linkages to economic growth.

5. This is fully detailed in chapter 5, and also in James W. Hughes and Joseph J. Seneca, *The Emerging Wealth Belt: New Jersey's New Millennium Geography* (Rutgers Regional Report Number 17, September 1999).

6. Joel Garreau, *Edge City: Life on the New Frontier* (New York: Doubleday, 1991).

7. The broad thirty-one-county Tri-State Region, centered on Manhattan and including portions of Connecticut, New Jersey, and New York, ultimately had a comprehensive regional mall grid comprising forty-seven million square feet of regional mall space located in forty-eight enclosed superregional malls. *See* James W. Hughes and George Sternlieb, *Retailing and Regional Malls* (Rutgers Regional Report Volume III, 1991).

8. The major nonsuburban office concentration in this trend was located on the Hudson River waterfront—New Jersey's Gold Coast, or "Wall Street West."

9. Alternatively, New Jersey's employment base was only 48 percent the size of New York City's.

10. In this chapter, the yearly employment figures that are used comprise annual averages. In other chapters, the yearly employment figures are measured from December to December in seasonally adjusted terms.

11. The demographic forces are also analyzed in James W. Hughes and Joseph J. Seneca, *Demographics, Economics, and Housing Demand* (Rutgers Regional Report Number 29, April 2012).

12. This period encompassed a tumultuous ride on the economic roller coaster. It started with the weak 2003–07 national employment expansion; it was then followed by the Great 2007–09 Recession and the less-than-great national employment recovery (2010–13). New York City's remarkable performance was partially assisted by the extensive federal rescue package that supported Wall Street and ameliorated the credit crisis.

CHAPTER 4   TRANSPORTATION AND THE ECONOMY

1. John T. Cunningham, *New Jersey: America's Main Road* (New York: Doubleday & Company, 1966), 53. According to Cunningham, this quote is usually credited to Benjamin Franklin, but it might have been James Madison.

2. Wheaton J. Lane, *From Indian Trail to Iron Horse* (Princeton, NJ: Princeton University Press, 1939).

3. "The years between 1800 and 1828 in New Jersey are called the 'Turnpike Era.' . . . During this time, 54 original charters were secured for turnpike companies in New Jersey, and about 550 miles of gravel and dirt were laid." Floyd W. Parsons, ed., *New Jersey: Life, Industries and Resources of a Great State* (Newark, NJ: New Jersey State Chamber of Commerce, 1928).

4. This history draws heavily on Edyth Hetman, *People—The Transportation Connection: A Brief History of the NJDOT* (Ewing, NJ: New Jersey Department of Transportation, 2001).

5. While the total toll-road mileage length is only about 16 percent of the more than 1,900 miles of the state highway system, the toll roads' strategic location in critical, demand-stressed transportation corridors and their multiple-lane configurations render their overall impact much greater than their length alone. In fact, their total lane mileage represents a much higher proportion of the lane mileage of the state highway system, where there still are a number of two-lane roadways.

6. Juliet Dellecker Michaelson, "Walk-and-Ride: How MidTown Direct Has Affected Residential Property Values within Walking

Distance of Train Stations" (master's thesis, Columbia University, New York, 2004).

7. Ridership on New Jersey Transit trains to Manhattan increased by over 50 percent between 1992 and 2000, while PATH ridership increased by 35 percent. And most of the new jobs added in Manhattan in the 1980s and 1990s were filled by commuters, not Manhattan residents. See Rosemary Scanlon and Edward S. Seeley Jr., *At Capacity: The Need for More Rail Access to the Manhattan CBD* (New York: New York University, Rudin Center for Transportation Policy & Management, 2004).

8. In addition, PATH service was also critical in providing access to the new office complexes.

CHAPTER 5   THE WEALTH BELT

1. The Southern Shore region, particularly number-one ranking Cape May County, represents a special situation. The valuation per capita calculation produces exaggerated results in seasonal areas, since the valuation of seasonal housing is included in the numerator, but only year-round residents are included in the denominator. This yields misleadingly high numbers.

2. Cape May County, as just noted, ranks number one, but it is a unique case.

3. The Bureau of Economic Analysis eliminated county-level employment after 2007. Thus, in table 5.11, the year 2007 is used instead of 2003. The 2011 data come from the U.S. Bureau of Labor Statistics.

CHAPTER 6   DEMOGRAPHY, THE ECONOMY, AND HOUSING

1. These are detailed in James W. Hughes and Joseph J. Seneca, eds., *America's Demographic Tapestry: Baseline for the New Millennium* (New Brunswick, NJ: Rutgers University Press, 1999).

2. More specifically, there were 998,000 dwelling units authorized by building permit in New Jersey between 1950 and 1970. No other period comes close to this level of production.

3. As noted in earlier chapters, we also use the term "millennials," although there is less agreement on the group's precise age delineation.

4. This record-breaking economic expansion started in March of 1991 and lasted a full ten years—120 months. It ended with a recession that began in March 2001.

5. In the year 2000, echo boomers were between five and twenty-three years of age.

6. In 2012, echo boomers were between seventeen and thirty-five years of age.

7. Almost 60 percent of total dwelling units authorized by building permit in New Jersey in 2012 were multifamily; only 40 percent were single-family. This is down from 73.5 percent single-family in 2002, and 86.5 percent in 1992. The share of new homes being built nationwide as rental apartments is at the highest level since a baby boom–inspired surge four decades ago.

8. Had the baby bust's age sector not been bolstered by immigration, the decline would have been on the order of 13 percent between 2000 and 2010. The same is true in the current decade (2010–20).

9. The Census Bureau classifies households into two broad groups: family and nonfamily households. "Families" consist of two or more related individuals. "Nonfamilies" consist of singles, or two or more unrelated individuals. "Families" are further subdivided into "married-couple families" (with or without children), or "other families" (male or female householders without spouses, with or without children).

10. In a shorter time frame, this percentage share is double that of 1960. Moreover, the 26 percent share in 2010 would have been higher in the absence of recession-induced "doubling-up" and/or young adults returning to, or remaining in, the parental hearth. This doubling-up will be reduced with economic recovery.

CHAPTER 7   NEW MILLENNIUM, NEW DYNAMICS

1. For the entire December 1939–December 1999 period, the average decade employment growth (private-sector) was 13.8 million jobs. During the December 1979–December 1999 period, the average decade growth was 18.0 million jobs. Between December 1999 and December 2009, 3.0 million jobs were lost.

2. December 1939 to December 1999.

3. This period encompassed a tumultuous ride on the economic roller coaster. It started with the weak 2003–07 national employment expansion; it was then followed by the Great 2007–09 Recession and the less-than-great national employment recovery (2010–13). New York City's remarkable performance was partially assisted by the extensive federal financial sector rescue package that supported Wall Street and ameliorated the credit crisis.

4. James Manyika, Michael Chui, Jacques Bughin, Richard Dobbs, Peter Bisson, and Alex Marrs, *Disruptive Technologies: Advances That Will Transform Life, Business, and the Global Economy* (Seoul, Korea: McKinsey & Company, McKinsey Global Institute, May 2013).

5. Antoinette Martin, "NJ Is Now Center of the 'Digital Universe,'" Globest.com, March 6, 2014.

6. The new Realogy building involved the renovation and expansion of an existing 225,000-square-foot Verizon call center to create the new 285,000-square-foot headquarters.

7. The other Alcatel-Lucent structures were demolished.

About the Authors

JAMES W. HUGHES, Distinguished Professor and dean of the Edward J. Bloustein School of Planning and Public Policy at Rutgers, The State University of New Jersey, is director of the Rutgers Regional Report and a nationally recognized expert on development patterns, housing and demographic trends, and regional economics. Dr. Hughes is the recipient of Rutgers' Richard P. McCormick Award for Excellence in Alumni Leadership; the Rutgers Presidential Award for Distinguished Public Service; the Warren Hill Award of the New Jersey Bankers Association for outstanding commitment and contributions to the banking industry; and the Distinguished Service Award of the New Jersey Chapter of the American Planning Association. Dean Hughes has been both a Woodrow Wilson and a Ford Foundation Fellow.

JOSEPH J. SENECA is University Professor of Economics within the Bloustein School at Rutgers University. Professor Seneca, a Phi Beta Kappa graduate of the University of Pennsylvania, holds a PhD in economics from that institution. He served as Rutgers' vice president for academic affairs and chief academic officer from 1991 through 2003. For many years Dr. Seneca served as chair of the New Jersey Council of Economic Advisors, a nonpartisan expert board that advised the state's governor and legislature. He is the author of several books on the economics of environmental quality and numerous articles and reports on state and local economic development. He received the Educator of the Year Award from the Research and Development Council of New Jersey and teaching and public service awards from the university.